Windows into My World

Latino Youth write Their Lives

edited by sarah cortez
with an introduction by virgil suárez

PIÑATA
BOOKS

PIÑATA BOOKS
ARTE PÚBLICO PRESS
HOUSTON, TEXAS

This volume is made possible through grants from the City of Houston through the Houston Arts Alliance and by the Exemplar Program, a program of Americans for the Arts in collaboration with the LarsonAllen Public Services Group, funded by the Ford Foundation.

Piñata Books are full of surprises!

Piñata Books
An imprint of Arte Público Press
University of Houston
452 Cullen Performance Hall
Houston, Texas 77204-2004

Cover art by Gustavo Bretones
Cover design by Giovanni Mora

Windows into My World: Latino Youth Write Their Lives / edited by
     Sarah Cortez.
          p.   cm.
     ISBN 978-1-55885-482-6 (alk paper)
          1. Hispanic Americans—Biography. 2. Youth—United States—
     Biography. 3. United States—Biography. I. Cortez, Sarah.
     E184.S75W56 2007
     305.235092'368073—dc22
     [B]
                                                       2006052470
                                                              CIP

♾ The paper used in this publication meets the requirements of the American National Standard for Information Sciences—Permanence of Paper for Printed Library Materials, ANSI Z39.48-1984.

7 8 9 0 1 2 3 4 5 6   10 9 8 7 6 5 4 3 2 1

Dedication

This book is dedicated firstly to Tatcho Mindiola, Ph.D., who believed in my dream of teaching undergraduates to write memoir, and secondly, to Nicolás Kanellos, Ph.D., who believed in my vision for this book.

contents

preface

THIS BOOK WAS BORN OUT OF A CLASS I taught for the Center for Mexican American Studies at the University of Houston – Central Campus. That class, entitled "Memoir and Mexican American Identity," was born out of a belief. That belief was the conviction that college undergraduates could learn to write compelling and complex literary memoir. That one didn't need to be middle-aged or beyond to make sense out of one's life experiences on the page in a way that would open one's own understanding while also engaging the reader in a fascinating journey.

Memoir demands a strong narrative thrust while also affording the writer the opportunity for self-reflection without the veil of fiction. It is necessary that the memoirist not only tell an interesting story, but also choose the story, decide which parts of the story to tell, select the most effective form, and show how this story functions in the writer's own current life. The last imperative is where the reader begins to know the author, and this is memoir's most radical act. By knowing the author, the reader comes to know, appreciate, and (in good memoir) understand a world different that his/her own.

As the students in that first class wrote and revised, I found myself falling in love with their imagery, their voices. When I heard the first versions of such stories as Nancy L. Avila's "El Saucito," Juanita Montoya's "She-Ra," and Maria Teresa Brothers' "Independence Battle," I knew I must create a book of many essays by young Latino students across the United States.

Five years later, we—the authors and I—have our book to share with you, our reader. There have been countless revisions, countless telephone calls and emails with my suggestions for revision and the authors' re-envisioned essays.

If one concurs with Ramón Saldívar on *Chicano Narrative: The Dialectics of Difference* in proposing that Mexican-American authors use narrative not only to illustrate or translate a particular exotic reality, but, more importantly, to embody new ways of perceiving social reality and significant changes in ideology, then the larger significance of personal writing becomes apparent, and the importance of listening to the self-recorded history of our young people becomes even more so.

The authors and I hope that many, many other young people will read these narratives and feel empowered to continue the ageless task of creating meaning out of life's events.

Sarah Cortez
Editor

introduction

THE FIRST THING THAT WILL STRIKE YOU about these memoir essays is how tender they are, and how raw. Raw in the good sense, as in alive, as in vital. As in REAL. The voices gathered in this volume you are clutching in your hands, dear reader, are a powerful testament to how Latino/a youth face the world, whether as immigrants, or as citizens of a vast country. A country, I must add, and—I speak from experience here—so vast, one can easily lose oneself forever.

I am certain that you will immediately be engaged by Nancy L. Avila's "El Saucito," the opening essay, but also "Lalito" by Claudia Balderas and "Güera" by Maria Teresa Brothers—and this is just the beginning of a wonderful collection of illuminating and rich voices. And reading through *Windows into My World: Latino Youth Write Their Lives*, I could not help but think about my life as both as a student and now a teacher of Latino/a kids at the universities . . . though still few and far between. (I teach in Florida where the Latino/a student population still does not reflect the overall numbers of Latino/a taxpaying residents in the State of Florida.)

I think about school because it is such an integral part of Latino/a youth experience, though perhaps you are already familiar with the bitter-edged, hardcore statistics that Latino/a kids have a fifty percent chance of dropping out of school. And most do, even when politicians continue to insist that everything can be made better (a tall tale I've been hearing politicians talk about for the last thirty years). Yes, I cannot help but think of all the children still left behind.

You read these memoirs and remember the way back through your own passing, your own youth and infancy here in the United States and, perhaps, back where your parents and family came from. And often, the story is not a pretty one. It is heart-wrenching, and filled with pain and fear.

I know that this was still the case back in my time when I attended first Henry T. Gage Junior High School and then later Huntington Park Senior High School in the white-flight city of Huntington Park, Los Angeles, California. It was a tough environment for any recently arrived immigrant like myself, and for my parents who would punch the clock in for about thirty years of factory work and piece-meal wages. I have to imagine that my junior and high school experience was in many ways no different than much of the experience the essays gathered here relate: an extreme longing to fit in, to be welcomed and wanted, to be a part of something larger than oneself. The American Dream — that gargantuan myth — would never be available to any of us, and least of all to our parents, as they struggled to keep us fed, clothed, and off to school.

These lucid, well-written pieces are about family, about identity, about finding your way into maturity . . . it's amazing how grown-up these teenagers and young adults sound to me. There's hope, I say, and you read these pieces and know it is true. There's lots of hope and help on the way. The new generations are making great strides. But also, they have not forgotten their place of roots, their blood connections back to place and family, and most of all, and also most importantly, they have not forgotten their Spanish, the language of their heritage. You will love "Do You Speak English?" by Maritza Santibáñez-Luna, where the ending resonates with "I belong here . . . The place has changed, but not the questions."

I predict you are going to love pieces like "Life by *Seventeen*" by Jynelle A. Gracia and "Matsuharu's Quest" by Victor Matsumura—wonderful, exciting pieces by writers who are already exhibiting a world of promise and talent. But such is the overall quality of the book. I am intrigued by this amazing need to speak, to be heard, to be read, that all these writers possess . . . which is a great sign of hope, I would like to believe.

It is extremely painful often to read a wonderful, awe-inspiring piece like Gina Taha's "Extranjero," and not feel the pangs of trying so hard to belong to a hostile place: be it New York, Miami, or Los Angeles, where again I grew up. These are young writers, true, most of them starting out by flexing their writing muscles already well-developed, with much to say about the worlds they traverse and live in on a daily basis. Already in their young lives, these writers have lived a lot, seen a lot, and learned much from their experiences, and again, the fact that they are brave enough to write about it is a great indication that perhaps not all is lost, that things are getting better.

And in fact they will, as more people learn to participate in the great democratic exchange provided by the Constitution of these United States. Our communities have learned, over time, to find their way to the voting booths. And great strides have been made to make a difference, to participate and to try to change the status quo.

The voices gathered here by the wonderful editorial eye of Sarah Cortez are not overtly political which is why I have brought up some political facts from my own life, but the seeds are there, imbedded in the writing, in the bold personal testaments each of these writers have given us as a gift.

I loved this collection, that much is obvious, but what I can guarantee you at the beginning of this amazing reading experience is that you are going to thoroughly enjoy the ride, and you will remember not only the stories, but also the young writers who speak so eloquently about their lives at such an essential rite of passage.

Virgil Suárez
Florida State University

El saucito

Nancy L. Avila

THE FIRST TIME I WENT TO "EL SAUCITO," I remember comparing it to the cemeteries of the United States. Instead of grass, it had gravel. Instead of simple headstones made of granite or marble, which give off a certain air of elegance, there were huge, gaudy, elaborate headstones with statues of the Virgin or of some other religious figure. The row of tombs in El Saucito seemed to go on forever and were so numerous that one could, and often did, forget where their loved ones rested. El Saucito was everything that I, at the age of eight, knew nothing of. It held pain, memories, and traditions, but most of all, it held history. History of a dry, mountainous land foreign to me. But, more importantly, this was the history of a family I never knew but treasured deeply.

Though I had seen her millions of times in pictures wearing the black lace rebozo around her head and shoulders and had heard about her many more times from my mother, to be standing in front of my great-grandmother's tomb was an intense moment filled with mixed feelings. Those mixed feelings came partly from being in such a sacred place, but mostly from seeing my mother mourn peacefully a loss that had occurred so long ago. I felt a strong connection with Florencia García and her sacred resting place.

"Mami, why did you love your Abuelita Flor so much?"

"Well, because she took care of me, and she was like my mother."

"Because your mom died when you were a baby, right?"

She didn't have to respond because I knew the answer; I had heard the story all through my childhood. Not only that, but I knew it by memory and repeated it to whoever asked me. "I only have one set of grandparents and they live in San Luis, that's in Mexico. My mom's mom died when she was three, and I don't know what happened to her dad." The truth was that I did know about my mother's father, but I hated to talk about it. I couldn't understand how someone could abandon his wife and kids. I didn't know much about my maternal grandparents, but I did know that Felipe Guerrero had a second family and Isabel Juarez, mother of four children and struck with ovarian cancer, was unknowingly the other woman. I was always so grateful to have both of my parents, and the thought of ever losing either one of them seemed so distant from me. My sisters and I were such carefree little girls who had our mother's used sewing machine to keep us "nice and frilly" and our father's booming voice to keep us protected and under control. There was never a Sunday that went by without our family talking, laughing, scolding—simply being a family—over hotcakes and *barbacoa*.

"That's right. I didn't know my mother because she died when I was three and I really don't have any memories of her. Abuelita Flor was my mother and I loved her very much and she loved me. Just like I love you girls."

"Did you care that you lost your father?"

"No, I didn't care because he was never there to begin with."

"Oh, how sad."

Even then, as a child, I felt it was a great loss not to care about a parent. Seeing my mother's indifference as she spoke about her father was an image ingrained in my mind. It was a feeling that I wanted no part of. Yet, I had nothing but unfeigned respect for her because I knew that growing up without a paternal figure in her life had made my mother somehow stronger. I could not imagine the dynamics behind this, but I knew it was true.

◆

My sisters and I were always surrounded by love. It wasn't anything that was said aloud, but rather felt through actions. Daddy's dark, sunburned face was always greeted with running laughter and "hello" kisses as soon as he walked through the door, and Mami's *caldo de pollo* was waiting for us daily after school no matter how much we loathed it because "cooked vegetables and chicken broth are good for the heart and soul." Good-night kisses from Mom's weary yet satisfied face were an every night ritual, as well as hugs on Christmas, birthdays, New Year's, and just about any other day that was celebrated. There were times, many times, when dark clouds seemed to reign over our home, but grudges were never kept. We were blessed by having such a strong foundation: a family who gave so much love even when times weren't always so happy. I loved my parents very much and felt that their love for us was even stronger. I believe that it is this love that creates strength. Strength to keep on living and loving and caring.

Although we continue to visit El Saucito every year, there is also another place we now visit. This place contains huge, ancient oak trees that create peace for the hundreds of marble and granite tombstones that line its elegant and flawlessly fresh-cut grass. There is no such thing as forgetting the exact location because the perfectly paved roads lead us to his final resting place. This place is Woodlawn, and it is frequented more than once a year. Woodlawn is my El Saucito. It too holds pain, memories, traditions, and the beginnings of my history. A history where, perhaps, my children can come and pay their respects to a grandfather they, too, never had a chance to meet. Woodlawn is everything that El Saucito was, but much closer than I ever wanted.

The night my father didn't come home was the first time I truly felt fear and uncertainty. The only life that I knew, a life of security and safety, of laughter and love, of fighting and then forgiving, vanished in one long, scary, lifeless night.

Killed. In a car crash.

His funeral was the first I had ever attended. I never imagined that I would be looking at his thick black eyebrows, long strong nose, and smooth brown skin thinking, *"Is this really the last time I am going to see you, Daddy? You can't even see me.*

You can't hear me say that I love you and that I need you to teach me how to drive and to give me permission to go out, and to yell at me when we don't agree, and to say that you're proud of me and to see me walk across the stage, and to walk me down the aisle . . . and . . . and . . . Who will do that now?"

Who will do that now?

From the moment he couldn't step into our home again and our silly kisses couldn't reach his face again, I knew deep down inside that I would have a place like El Saucito of my own. As a young child, I couldn't begin to comprehend the loss of a loved one; I could only try. As a sixteen-year-old girl, my life was turned upside down and suddenly immersed in a loss greater than I could possibly imagine.

Now I, too, mourn like my mother. I feel the pain and understand the ironic twist that life brings. Nothing is ever perfect for too long. I, too, share with my mother the loss of a parent. However, unlike her, I do care. And I care even more because she has to share my pain as well. A pain not only as great as mine, but also sadder.

gabriel

georgina baeza

ALAMEDA RUNS THROUGH EL PASO FROM EAST TO WEST. It's one of those major streets that takes you from the farthest end of El Paso to downtown. It divides El Paso into north and south. And it drew a line between the kids that went to Pasodale Elementary School.

There weren't too many of us who lived on the north side of Alameda. Usually parents on that side enrolled their kids at Marion Manor Elementary, so they wouldn't have to cross a busy street. After the final bell, those who lived on the north side of Alameda walked through the yellow-grassed field that was used for every outdoor school event. We'd all cross Alameda together and disperse after reaching Helm St.

There were only three of us who had to walk the two miles to the cream-colored brick apartments with red-orange roof shingles on Carpenter Street. It was there that the three of us had met. I had lived there before anyone else. My family moved there the summer before I began third grade when the landlord kicked us out of the three-bedroom home on Beatrix Street because Dad never paid the rent on time. Lizette came next. We met in Mrs. Yeager's third grade class, but didn't talk much because she was one of the popular girls. She had shoulder-length hair with bangs that she curled every morning with her mom's curling iron. She always wore blue jeans and shocking white Keds. I, on the other hand, was overweight with long brown hair and had to wear the clothes my mom made for me with the bargain fabric she bought downtown. Toward the end of that school year, Gabriel moved in when his mom broke up with her boyfriend. Gabriel was a year younger than Lizette and I, and we liked to say we only befriended him because of Ruby, his cousin.

The first time I met him, I knew we would be good friends. It was an early spring evening when the trees are just beginning to bud and the miniscule leaves are the color of a yellow-green Crayola. I had gone outside to see if anyone was playing kick-ball. Ruby was sitting at the bottom of the stairs that led up to her apartment. I went over to see if maybe she wanted to play.

I noticed a boy wearing a purple T-shirt with folded-up sleeves, black jeans that had knife-sharp creases straight down the front, and black cowboy boots climbing the guardrail to Ruby's stairs. He'd get up to the highest point and climb back down as he serenaded the neighborhood with his rendition of "I'm Proud to Be an American."

When Ruby noticed I was staring, she said, "That's my cousin Gabriel," then she turned to Gabriel and said, "Gabriel, this is Georgina."

Hearing this introduction, he quickly climbed back down, extended his hand to me, and said, "Hi, good to meet you."

I looked at his extended hand and remembered it was the signal for a handshake. I shook his hand and said, "Nice to meet you too."

"I'm gonna be living here soon."

"Really?" I asked.

"Yeah, he and his mom are getting an apartment here," Ruby interjected.

A few weeks later, Gabriel and his mom moved in. She worked at the Tonka factory near Cielo Vista Mall. Gabriel and I would usually play with the toys his mom bought at the employee discount store. My favorite were the camouflage-colored walkie-talkies, which we often used the summer after he moved in. We'd take them with us when we'd cross the dusty, empty lot to get to Ray's Beer Depot to buy our favorite treat—

big, green, tart pickles from the clear jar next to the cash register.

The next school year, Gabriel and I always walked to and from school together. Lizette would walk home with us whenever her aunts couldn't watch her after school, but she never walked to school because her mom always drove her. Although Lizette hardly ever acknowledged me at school, she always joined the evening kickball games at our apartments. Sometimes she even said I was her best friend, but I knew better.

At the beginning of sixth grade, Lizette's mom finished her police training, and with her new job she was able to afford a brand-new quadruplex apartment on the upper-east side of town. Lizette would no longer attend Pasodale and would soon forget about Gabriel and me.

In seventh grade, my parents split up, and I moved in with my oldest sister miles away from Carpenter Street. But before the last truckload of stuffed animals in Hefty bags and clothes still on hangers pulled out of the driveway, Gabriel and I promised each other we'd always be friends and do our best to keep in touch. To seal our promise, we walked over to the empty lot behind the apartments and buried a plastic Coke bottle full of sand.

During our sophomore year of high school, we became inseparable. Even though we still lived on different sides of town and went to different schools, we'd call each other every day and meet at the mall or downtown on Saturdays to window-shop and catch up on gossip.

It was almost midnight on a stormy summer desert night after our sophomore year when the telephone rang. "Hello," I muttered sleepily into the receiver.

"Hey."

"Hey, what's up?" I asked as I got off the couch to see if it was raining or just thundering.

"Nothing. What are you doing?"

"Well, I *was* sleeping."

"But it's still so early."

"I know, but I'm so tired. I had to get up at eight for registration."

"Oh yeah, that was today for you guys."

"Yeah."

"Have you heard the new Madonna song?"

"No, I don't think so."

"You want me to sing it to you?"

"No thanks, I'm sure I'll catch the video on MTV."

"Fine . . . Hey, I need to tell you something."

"About what?" I asked, hoping that he wasn't going to tell me that his mom was getting back together with Oscar, her ex-boyfriend who despised Gabriel.

"Remember that time I told you Mike tried to kiss me and I pushed him away?" he asked with a slight quiver in his voice.

"Yeah," I said a little relieved.

"Well, I didn't push him away, we kissed . . . and I really liked it . . . and he's kind of my boyfriend now. But you're the only one I've told, so please don't tell anyone especially not my mom. She'll kick me out."

"You know I won't tell."

"Yeah . . . Are you sure you still want to be my friend?"

"Yes! I'm not gonna stop being your friend because of that."

And it was true; I knew he needed me as much as I had needed him the summer before sixth grade when my brothers and sister moved out leaving me alone with my parents. Besides, I wasn't exactly shocked because he was the same guy who had always wanted to play with Barbies when he was over at my house. Plus, he went to great pains to appear as a real woman every Halloween.

I never told his mom his secret. Instead, I listened to him when he'd call me in the middle of the night panicking because he thought his mom might have seen him kissing Mike when he had dropped him off after their date. Later that summer, he and his mom were sitting at their kitchen/dining room table drinking strawberry-kiwi wine coolers after she got off work. I don't know if it was the wine coolers or if he was sick of the lies, but he told her, and all she said was, "Now I finally have the daughter I always wanted."

Eventually, his mom did kick him out because she got back together with Oscar. After living with Mike, then his own grandma, and later his older brother, Gabriel moved in with Alex or "the love of his life," as he once described him to me. One day while he was in town, he visited me and told me that he'd moved away to Seattle with Alex. Gabriel was working as a drag queen, which explained the heavy makeup, perfectly shaped eyebrows, and the long, manicured nails. He smiled as he showed off the thick, white-gold band Alex had put on his finger.

I wish we could have kept in touch, but it seems that friendships crumble when we've done all we can for each other. We lost touch when I began my senior year in high school and had to work weekends. I didn't have the time to join him at the drink-and-drown parties at the numerous nightclubs on Avenida Juárez. But when I remember all the pickles we shared, the way we held hands when we went to see my aunt Bucha laying in her ice-pink casket at her rosary, and the many nights we drove downtown to quench his curiosity about drag queens rumored to work the streets near the O.P. nightclub, I'm just glad I had him as a friend. Every time I think of him, I see him in a sunny apartment somewhere on the west coast of California, wrapped in a white bathrobe like the kind you get in those fancy hotels, sipping on a glass of red wine as he puts on his makeup before going out. When he's done with his makeup, he picks up the phone. Dials. It rings on my end, and I hear him say, "Hey, have you heard the latest . . .?"

Mis ojos

WHEN MY MOM WENT INTO LABOR in the early hours of that Sunday morning, my dad was nowhere to be found. He didn't even know that I had been born until a day later. When he came home, he found my brother Jorge and my sister Gabi, who were nine and ten, in his and mom's bedroom with the chest of drawers face down on the floor and the rug pulled back. Infuriated that they had discovered his money stash, he asked them what they were doing. They replied, "Looking for money to pay the hospital bill to bring home our baby sister." Instead of yelling at them, Dad helped them count the money they had found.

When I was a little girl, my dad used to call me *mis ojos*, my eyes. I was the youngest of his four children with my mom. Since I had been born on Father's Day in Mexico, June 15th, he always told me I had been his gift that year. Even though he sometimes spent way too much time with his good friend, Old Crow Whiskey, and didn't come home for days, he always remembered *mis ojos*.

If a little girl riding in his taxi left behind her plush puppy-dog purse, he always took it home, and as soon as he walked through the door, he searched for me in our two-bedroom mansion to give me my present. During those rare El Paso desert rainstorms, I was the only one who could wake him up to ask for a ride to school without being scolded and have two chilled quarters for the bus from the front left pocket of his jeans dropped into my warm pudgy hand. In sixth grade, when I decided that I wanted to play the trumpet in the school band, he spent three days in his sky-blue taxicab to make enough money to buy my trumpet.

Prior to my twelfth birthday, he asked my mom to find out what was on my wish list. When she told him, he went to the insignificant watch shop downtown wedged between the perfume shop and the cash exchange place and bought me the watch that I had asked for, and as an added bonus, he got me an airbrushed T-shirt with a slobbering Odie, Garfield's nemesis, and my name done in bright red letters like the kind you see on a pack of Bubble Yum. The T-shirt didn't fit and my name was misspelled, but I wore it anyway. It was the first time my dad had given me a birthday present and I didn't want him to think I didn't like it.

After my evening excursions in the neighborhood with my friends, I'd often find him leaning on his car in the parking lot in front of our apartment in the white, V-neck undershirt he'd worn that day and worn pajama bottoms, barefoot, with a pint of whiskey wrapped in a brown paper bag. Depending on his mood, he might call me over, and in a slurred voice, he'd say, *"Tú eres mis ojos, m'ija."* I would stand there hoping that my friends hadn't overheard him as they walked toward their own apartments. It was enough that my friends knew he was my dad; they didn't need to know his special nickname for me.

One Sunday morning toward the end of seventh grade, I came home to find my sister at our apartment loading my mattress along with my mom's onto her old Chevy truck. By the end of the day, all of our belongings were at my sister's house. From then on, Christmas cards would no longer be addressed to Filemon H. Baeza and Family.

A few months after my sister had moved us out from Dad's, as I was sitting on a slab of concrete that would later be my sister's garage, watching the sun set over the mountains, I saw a car approaching. As it drew closer to the house, I recognized it as my dad's taxi. I felt my stomach sink and my face grow pale. I wanted to see my dad but I was scared. There were so many stories of dads kidnapping their daughters and going to Mexico, but I was even more afraid of what he might tell me. I didn't want him to ask me if I missed him because that would make me cry and my whole tough girl cover would be blown. My sister, after seeing my reaction, went to find out what he wanted as I hid under my mom's dining room table, which had been placed outside until we either sold it or moved out. When she came back, she told me he had something for me.

"Can't he just give it to you?" I asked.

"No, he wants to give it to you," she replied.

My dad, as an experienced taxi driver, had all the patience in the world. I knew he wouldn't go away until he gave me whatever it was he had for me. I came out from under my hiding place and with strained steps walked toward his taxi. Wearing a yellow shirt and dark blue jeans that had been to the cleaners, he stepped out of the car. The smell of his Brut aftershave hung in the air. No whiskey. His face was puffy and rejuvenated from a good night's sleep. There was no way this was the same man rumored to be spending his days drunk and passed out near the Santa Fe Bridge with the homeless.

"How are you?" he asked.

"Okay."

"Here," he said as he handed me an envelope made out of powder-blue gas station napkins, "this is for you."

"Thanks," I said as I stood there holding the makeshift envelope, wanting to see the contents but too shy and embarrassed to open it.

"Are you going back to Pasodale next year?"

"No, Mom put me in Sanchez Middle School because it's closer and I can ride the bus."

"When do you start?"

"Next month. It's year 'round."

"You doing alright?"

"Yeah."

"That's good. Well, I have to get to work. Take care, *m'ija*."

"You too, Dad."

After he was gone, I walked back to the place where I'd been sitting before his visit, feeling less tense with a slight carefree bounce in my steps. My sister who was watching the entire visit asked me what was in the napkins. "I don't know," I said as I unfolded the napkins and found ten crisp twenty-dollar bills.

◆

My sister Gabi and I were on I-10 headed west under the dusty rain clouds outside of Ft. Hancock when my cell phone rang. "Hello?"

"Georgina," said Jorge.

"Yeah, what's up?"

"Mom just called . . . Dad's dead," he said with no feeling in his voice.

Georgina Baeza

"Okay, well, we're just outside of Ft. Hancock. We'll be there in about two hours. We're going straight to the hospital," I said in the same tone as his.

"Okay, I'll let Mom know."

"Okay, bye."

I turned to Gabi sitting in the driver's seat and gave her the news. I watched tears well up behind her bottom lashes as large grimy drops of rain hit the windshield.

When he departed, I was in the same place he had been when I arrived: absent. All the rushed packing that morning and speeding through San Antonio rainstorms seemed useless at that moment because I hadn't made it in time to see him living one last time.

When I arrived at the hospital hours after my brother's phone call, his body laid there on an intensely white hospital sheet. He looked just as I had seen him that evening at my sister's house: serene. There was no evidence of the past on his face. As I held his icy cold, bruised hand in mine, I realized that there were a lot of things about my dad that I had never understood, like why he had given me that money outside of my sister's house or why he had never stopped drinking. There were so many stories my dad would not be able to tell me—why he was court-marshaled or about his days as a race-car driver. But none of that mattered because to him no matter where he was, I was always *mis ojos*.

peach plug-ins

I'M GUESSING IT WAS AROUND 1992 when Glade Plug-Ins first hit the market. It was a pretty innovative idea since the sprays and carpet deodorizers didn't work. This new product promised to produce an aromatic smell for up to six weeks in any room, as long as the plastic adapter was plugged into the wall and a fragrance pack was inserted.

Around the same time, my life felt like a roller-coaster car going down a big dip. First, my brothers, Filly and Jorge, left home the day before my twelfth birthday. Filly had just obtained his truck driving license, and the job he had found wanted him to leave as soon as possible. I had known Jorge would leave because he had enlisted in the Army the year before he graduated from high school. My sister Gabi moved out that September because we lived too far away from the university. Since she didn't have a car, it would be easier for her to get her own place in that area. One of my close friends moved away later that fall. Then my dad decided that he would give sobriety a try. When he'd get home from work, instead of a bottle of whiskey in a wrinkly brown paper bag, he would walk in with a big brown paper bag with grease spots from the *pan dulce*. Even though I should have been happy that my siblings were out on their own, that my parents were not fighting, and that my best friend was happy at her new school, I didn't like the way things were. There had been too many changes in too little time.

Dad's sober period didn't last too long. About two months later, he was back on his "liter a day" plan. Filly came back home sometime in November because the effects of pot were much better than his biweekly thousand-dollar checks. In February, Mom got a job as a live-in caregiver for a woman who had been diagnosed with Alzheimer's disease. Mom's new job paid three times more than cleaning houses.

During that time, it was my ritual to cry from the time Mom left for work on Sundays until I passed out in front of the thirteen-inch, black-and-white television in my room. It was tough being in a house with these two men who could go from family to stranger in a shot or a hit; so I spent most of my time locked in my room eating anything I could get my hands on and watching television.

In April, Jorge was due for a month-long visit before the Army sent him to Korea for the last years of his time in the service. I hadn't seen much of him in the past year. Every time he'd come home on leave, it would only be for the weekend, and he would spend most of his time with his girlfriend. Within the last few months, they had broken up because Jorge found out that she had been cheating on him with one of his close friends. I was glad they had broken up because that meant he'd spend more time with me.

Jorge was my favorite brother, and, in some ways, he still is. When I was in kindergarten, he would walk me to school and kiss my pink, chubby cheeks, even if his friends were around. When he was in high school, he would save his daily bus fare all week so that he had money for his downtown shopping trips with his best friend Louie. Oftentimes, he would spend his savings on a new pair of polyester pants in size 14 petite for my mom or a 100-pack of markers for me from *la tienda de los chinos*.

The Christmas before his month-long visit he wasn't able to make it home because he was saving up for a car. However, he sent a big box full of presents for everyone. I found a small box about the size of a Band-Aid tin wedged between presents for my nieces. When I opened it on Christmas Day, I discovered a Mickey Mouse watch with a brown wrist strap, a white face, and a Mickey Mouse in the middle of it whose arms were used to point to the hour and the minute. It also had two little buttons on the outside of the face that caused it to play *It's a Small World* and the *Mickey Mouse Club* theme song. I remember being so thrilled because Jorge always thought about me. I couldn't wait for him to arrive.

Jorge was driving his metallic-blue, super VW Beetle from Ft. Campbell, Kentucky to El Paso. He was arriving the week after my spring break, so I spent the week of spring break cleaning and scrubbing carpets, trying to get rid of the stench that my brother and father produced with their respective habits. I even walked to the little corner store near San José Catholic Church and bought a box of German chocolate cake mix because I knew that was Jorge's favorite. Despite all my efforts, I couldn't get rid of the smell.

When Jorge finally arrived the Sunday afternoon after spring break, I was so relieved. I no longer had to spend my Sunday evenings alone. I wouldn't cry that evening or for the rest of that month. We would have to share a room because he could no longer share a room with Dad. It would be like a slumber party because we were sharing Mom's and my room. His Army-issued duffle bag served as a reminder that I was not alone when he was out with his friends or Gabi. It was especially nice to wake up and not see an empty bed across from me, but the best thing about having him home was that he always managed to make me laugh. Out of all of my siblings, I had always thought he was the funniest.

There were so many Saturday nights that he would call while he was doing overnight guard duty to make extra money, and we would spend about an hour laughing so hard that neither of us could breathe. Once we got started, it was hard to stop. Sometimes my mom listened in and other times she would pick up the other phone and say, *"¡Ya cuelgen! Jorge, te va a salir bien grande el bil."*

We would say we were going to get off, but then I'd do the raspy horse laugh that he loved and there we went again for another half hour. During his visit, there were so many nights we did this. There was no mom to make us get to sleep and no *bil* to worry about.

Soon after his arrival, we drove over the lumpy hills of Yarbrough Street to Wal-Mart on a little shopping trip. As we were walking through the aisles crowded with shopping carts and people, he mentioned our foul-smelling apartment. When we reached the cleaning supplies aisle, he threw a few peach nectar plug-ins into the shopping cart. Among them was one of the night-light versions shaped like a teddy bear with stars on its tummy where the smell would flow out. I don't know if he chose that one for me, but that was the plug-in that I would keep in my room until I moved away for college.

When I'm at Wal-Mart smelling the different plug-ins and run into a pack of sweet-smelling peach nectar, the smell takes me back to Jorge's visit and all the things that came after, like my parents' inevitable separation. I sometimes consider buying that scent, but always put the package back on the shelf for the next time. If my house always smelled of peach nectar, it might cause me to replace the memories that saunter back with this smell. Although most of these memories are bittersweet, I prefer to keep them intact.

Lalito

claudia Balderas

THE DAY MY UNCLE AND AUNT, Jorge and Laura, married is a day
I will forever remember. I must have been around thirteen or so.
Coming from an extensive family, weddings, and any other celebration for that matter, have always been considered perfectly
good opportunities to come together and catch up with each
other's lives. And this wedding was no exception. We were
going to Monterrey! I was thrilled. The entire family had decided to attend: uncles, aunts, grandparents, and cousins, as well as
their uncles, aunts, grandparents, and cousins. It was the perfect
occasion to see all those I had not seen in such a long time: a
family reunion.

The wedding was beautiful; everything about it was stun-
ning. Not a single detail had been overlooked. It was also excep-
tionally formal. I don't think I had ever been to such an elegant
wedding. Everyone was dressed in their best. All the men wore
fitted black suits and tuxedos that made them look as if they had
all the money in the world. The women wore silky colorful
dresses that glistened and sparkled as they walked by. The
reception hall was dark with only a small candle lighting each
table. There were waiters who served the most delicious foods
and desserts (my favorite being a *tres leches* cake) and who
brought us all the Cokes we wanted. Of course, we had to limit
ourselves. "Drinking too much will make you want to go to the
restroom a lot, and we don't want to spend the whole night in
there," my aunts explained.

We, the children, were told to act our best and behave ourselves or we would have to face the consequences when we got home. *No se chiflen* (Don't misbehave), we heard constantly before arriving. Yet, to everyone's surprise, we all behaved. After all, there was no need to misbehave; we were simply excited to see each other. So instead, and as an act of courtesy and respect for the magnificent festivity, we opted to act like grown-ups and to enjoy the exquisite celebration that was before us.

Everything was going as planned. The food was great, all of it. The band kept everyone, even us kids, entertained. The wedding was perfect from beginning to end. Or so we thought. Little did we know what was about to happen. Things began to get a little crazy and out of line when one of my uncles, Tío Lalo, a tough and strong man, after having had a little too much to drink, began to cry all of a sudden. He had been drinking all night long, enjoying himself and dancing the night away. I suppose his soft side came out once he reached his top level of drinking. He stumbled over to my grandmother, his mother, hugged her tightly, and began to cry, like a little kid. He begged my grandmother to forgive him for a bunch of things he had apparently done in his life. He kept saying he was sorry. I assumed it was probably because he beat his brothers and sisters up a lot as a kid. He was never quite the good child of the family. Rumor has it, though, that it was more than just that. My grandmother, a stocky yet frail woman, puzzled and somewhat embarrassed, tried to back him away and assured him things were okay. She told him that he had nothing to be sorry for. She couldn't believe that my uncle had chosen this very moment to make a fool out of himself and to bring her down with him. My uncle's wife, Tía Sara, awfully embarrassed, tried to pull him away. "Lalito, *ya*," she kept saying, delicately grabbing on to his suit and looking around, adjusting her tight gold dress every time he pushed her away, hoping that no one was watching. Still, my uncle was determined to hold on to my grandmother for the rest of the night, a spectacle that could not be overlooked.

Everyone who attended saw what happened, even the bride and groom. Some giggled at the humorous scene, while others whispered into other people's ears to look at the crying, drunken man who was clinging onto the old lady in the purple dress. I remember watching from a distance, standing in the doorway of the reception hall with my cousins, our mouths wide open. We could not believe our eyes. We cracked up laughing, my cousins and I, thinking my uncle had gone crazy. We could not take in the fact that we had all tried to behave ourselves as best we could and yet there was my uncle, a grown-up, who could not control his behavior. I don't think I had ever seen a drunken person before. Sure, I had seen them on television, but never in real life. And this was certainly not how I imagined a drunken man, especially not one like my uncle. It was fascinating to see how my uncle's drunkenness had allowed him to reveal his true inner feelings and how, instead of showing his drunkenness as a macho man would, he opted to show it by publicly weeping.

Mi tío Lalo. My uncle Lalo. My perception of him was forever changed at that instant. He was no longer that tough, dark-skinned Mexican macho that came home every evening sweating from a hard day's work and smelling like the cheap beer he bought at the corner store on his daily walk home. No. This was something I would never forget and haven't to this day. Whenever I think of my uncle, I see a kid, a child, a person with real emotions and a heart, a big heart, so big it was willing to open itself up in front of an immense audience.

I wonder if my uncle remembers this or not. Perhaps he has forgotten. Children, however, never forget those things that greatly impact them. I know I haven't forgotten this incident. Why? I don't know. Perhaps I was searching for that something that would tell me once and for all that "Lalito" was human and that there was more to him than just toughness and roughness. And I realized at that very moment that there most definitely was.

Almost Dead

"OH, DEAR GOD! I'm going to die! This is it! Oh man!"

I had never been as close to death as I was the day I visited a *feria*, the Mexican version of a carnival, in Río Bravo, a small town in the state of Tamaulipas, in Mexico. It was the summer of 1998. At the age of fourteen, I was still enthralled with my family's yearly visit to the well-known *feria* that travels through many parts of Mexico and provides wholesome family entertainment together with an out-of-this-world circus experience and a series of concerts. It was customary for the *feria* to come to the Mexican border town of Reynosa, my hometown, every year. However, an educational institute had been built on the grounds where the *feria* was usually held, so this would be the first year the *feria* would not be providing fun and entertainment to the people of Reynosa.

"It's okay," my father told both my brother and I. "We'll go to the one in Río Bravo. It's only about forty-five minutes away." And so we took off, my family and I, together with an uncle and my self-acclaimed oh-so-cool cousin Hugo. It was especially exciting to have Hugo along for the trip, who, at sixteen, was a charmer to all the girls and the envy of every guy. He dressed in tight shirts that complemented his thin figure. He wore the coolest dark glasses and handmade accessories, sold in the small markets of Reynosa, which gave him an exotic look like he had just come straight from Hollywood.

Upon arriving, I thought to myself, "This is going to be awesome!" We decided to first visit the circus, a five-star circus by Mexican standards, and then play some games, from which I won absolutely nothing. By the time we decided to get on the rides, nighttime had fallen. Yet the quiet town of Río Bravo, with the *feria*'s many colorful lights illuminating the sky and the numerous stereos playing *cumbias* and *rancheras* at full blast, was yet to fall asleep.

"Llévese dos por diez," a dark man shouted, telling us to take two of his displayed products for ten pesos. I smiled at the man, as he held out a piece of colorful homemade candy on each hand, and kept walking. While we were all trying to figure out which ride to get on, I noticed that all of the rides' plugs and cables were scattered throughout the *feria's* floor. "This is dangerous," I told my mother, as I reached to grab her delicate hand. "Anybody can step on these and easily cause a spark or can make a ride stop."

"Don't be silly," my mother replied. "That's not going to happen."

As I tried to console myself with my mother's reply, I could not help but think of myself getting stuck on a ride because of a broken cable. I had been told many times that I was *una escandalosa*, the Spanish term for a drama queen, always making a big deal about everything. Yet the thought of my life ending on a ride made me grow very hesitant and nervous. And so I decided not to ride anything to keep myself on the safe side.

Not much time had passed when Hugo walked over to me, placed one hand on my shoulder, and coolly proposed to get on a ride with me.

"*Ándale,* Claudia," he said, pointing to a rocket ship-like ride that went in loops and had people screaming at the top of their lungs. I wanted to say no, but how could I say no to the person I thought was the coolest guy in the world? *He* was asking *me* to get on a ride with him. Surely, if he thought it was okay to get on the ride, I had no reason to worry. Plus, I didn't want to look like a wimp in front of my cousin who I admired so much and only saw on a few occasions. I knew, too, that if I said yes to him I could maybe, just maybe, become a part of Hugo's cool clique, and then he would invite me to all the parties he went to and I would surely get to meet all his cute friends that were pictured in his many photo albums. And so I proceeded to get into what seemed to be the scariest ride in the world.

The rocket ship was divided into boxes with only two people per box. I stepped into my seat and held on tightly to the cold metal bars. The man who operated the ride stopped in front of us, buckled us up, and closed the box. A rush of excitement went through my body as the ride began. After what seemed to be only a few seconds, I found myself screaming along with everyone else on the ride. True, it was scary, but it was also very exhilarating. I laughed and screamed as I closed my eyes and opened them only to see the world upside down.

Then, halfway through the ride, the ship gave a half loop and suddenly stopped in midair, leaving everyone upside down. As my head dangled, I couldn't help but wonder if my worst fear had actually come true. I blocked my mind from everything around me and tried not to let the screaming get me into panic mode. But then I did something I know now I should not have done—I looked over at my cousin. Hugo, my valiant cousin who was never bullied by anyone, had fear written all over him. His face had lost its light brown complexion and had been replaced by a reddish-purple color. He had an anguished look that freaked me out. "*Ay, Dios mío,*" I thought to myself, as I tried to pick my head up. I felt as if all the blood in my body had rushed into my face and it made me feel hot and dizzy.

Then, after what seemed to be the longest seconds, maybe even minutes of my life, the ride resumed. I felt relief to know that I was still alive, but I wanted the ride to stop then and there. I was young and couldn't take the pressure. I felt like throwing up. I wanted to get out, run to my parents' arms, and tell them what had just happened. I wanted to confirm that it was all true and not just a product of my imagination.

I was quiet as I left the ride; I didn't want Hugo to know how scared I had been. I knew he had been scared himself but wouldn't dare tell me. His pride always came first and so I said nothing to him. I explained to my mother what had happened, and, to my surprise, her reaction was that I was crazy. "It's all in your head," she told me, and I wondered if that was true. Was it really all my head? Had I let my paranoia get to me? No, this was real, I concluded. My mother saw nothing, so her opinion was not valid. We all knew the danger of rides in Mexico. They were not safe like the rides in Astroworld or Disney World. These were cheap rides made only for those who were willing to risk their lives in them. I stood in the parking lot as we were getting ready to leave, pissed off at the men who had created such an unsafe situation.

I remember the ride back that night. My little brother, filled with excitement, talked and talked to my uncle and my parents about all the fun he had experienced that day, while Hugo smiled at him but said nothing. I looked outside the window and fixed my eyes on the flat land and the few trees we passed by on that deserted highway leading us back to Reynosa. I ignored all the fun and excitement I had experienced that day and focused only on that one incident. Occasionally, I would glance at my cousin, looking for an expression that would tell me he had been as freaked out as I was. He gave me nothing. He didn't even utter a single word to me. "Idiot," I thought to myself as I closed my eyes to fall asleep, knowing I would never again beg my parents to take my brother and I to that annual *feria* I had so much loved. And knowing, too, that I would never again do anything to try to please my "cool" cousin Hugo.

claudia вalderas

güera

María Teresa Brothers

THERE IS A LITTLE TOWN CALLED IXTAPA, near the coast in the state of Jalisco, Mexico. My family and I moved there when I was four because it was the closest town to my dad's work at the time and the only place available to live. Around that time, Ixtapa was just "a fly speck on the map," as my dad once described it to my brother Martin, to encourage him to expand his knowledge somewhere outside the town's limits. My brother, like many others raised there, thinks he knows everything. But, for example, he doesn't know that people may put pepper on the table while having a meal. "People don't put pepper on the table, just salt," Martin furiously argued with my dad once before dinner. Martin was being really serious. He went on and on for so long with brisk gestures insisting he was right that I almost believed him.

At that time, Ixtapa had just one unfinished church, one middle school and one elementary school near the church and in front of La Plaza. La Plaza was the most popular place, or, may I say, the only place, to go on Sundays to walk and meet friends while the band's playing resounded in our ears. Most of the people knew each other, especially those families who had been living there since the town was founded with the Montgomery Company and its banana plantations. Older people recognized you by your family's last name, or, if not, at least they tried to fit you into categories by the *colonia* or neighborhood you lived in. People could walk everywhere in town due to the short distances from one place to another. The only buses went to Puerto Vallarta, the closest city in the area.

In a small town in Mexico like this, there are just a few light-skinned people. Since my color is white, I was called *güera* (which means light-skinned in Spanish) by most of the people who didn't know my name. "Güera!" I would hear from someone who was trying to catch my attention when I was walking down the street. I just pretended it wasn't me being called until I recognized somebody friendly enough to talk to.

On the one hand, I understood that it is very common to be given a nickname based on some particular part of one's appearance, but on the other hand, this nickname sounded really pejorative. Anyway, there was nothing that I could have done to change my appearance or to change what people call me, but it was a crude reminder that I was an outsider because of my skin color.

What I didn't understand was that I was often confused with another girl, another *güera*. There was this girl named Brenda, and in almost everyone's opinion she looked like my twin. I never really hung out with her, and I think that's probably why nobody really took a look at us up close at the same time to realize that we didn't look alike. We were only the same age and the same color, but that was it. We didn't have similar eyes, noses, or mouths. But to most of the people in Ixtapa, we looked alike because we were different from them. People would even come up to me confusing me with her, calling me by her name. Everyone in town would do it: a teacher at my school, people in my neighborhood, and once, even her own brother! Our conversations sounded something like this:

"No, you are making a mistake, I'm not her," I would say.

"Is she your sister?" they would ask.

"No, she is not my sister, and we are not related."

She didn't seem bothered about the situation like I was.

◆

Ixtapa is not as small as it used to be because a lot of new-comers have moved there bringing more diversity in people's skin tones. I have come to realize that people take a bus to go from one part of the town to another. Ixtapa finally has more than one church and an elementary school in each of the major sections of the town. My little town is becoming more and more urbanized, so people hardly know each other anymore. When I have the opportunity to go back there, I'm amazed by the changes I see. La Plaza was remodeled about four years ago against a lot of people's wishes. I saw a pile of rocks sitting in front of La Plaza, and I realized that was my old school being rebuilt. Ixtapa has changed, and the people recall the past with nostalgia after seeing their old plaza and school replaced by new ones. Even if the changes are really major, like seeing new hous-es and new little stores in the streets, I'm positive one thing will not change and that is that I will hear someone trying to get my attention, "Hey, güera!" I don't think I will be bothered as much as it used to bother me. Even some close friends in Ixtapa have started calling me that too. Now I feel like they really know me, and I like the way the nickname sounds.

A foreign Holiday

November 1999
IT'S THE FIRST TIME I see Houston like this. My dad drives along FM 1960 looking for an appealing restaurant everybody agrees on. Nothing. The street is quiet and empty, with no signs of OPEN anywhere. It seems that we are the only ones out trying to get something to eat at a decent time in the afternoon. I have not had breakfast, waiting to go out to lunch with my family. But I also had no other choice since there is nothing edible at my house but the leftovers of some food we ate a week ago.

"What is going on?" I say.

"There should be something open somewhere," my dad replies, already tired of driving for what seems like an hour. His face is sweating with a question mark on his forehead trying to find an answer to this nonsense.

"I'm hungry. I can eat anything."

"Me too," my brother agrees with my mom.

I'm irritated and starving. It seemed a good idea to eat out because my dad has the day off, and my brother and I don't have classes. We don't know anybody yet and we really don't have any friends. We just have each other.

"It's Thanksgiving!" my dad says, and we look at each other's eyes wondering what that really means and why it has such an impact on a big city like Houston.

◆

This first Thanksgiving in Houston was a disaster. We couldn't find any grocery stores or restaurants open, so we ended up at a gas station buying bread and ham to make some untasty sandwiches later. I hadn't heard much about this "Thanksgiving holiday" in Mexico. There we celebrated *Navidad, El Día de los Muertos,* or *El Día de la Independencia,* but were mostly unaware of foreign traditions. I once had heard my American cousin saying something about it, but she'd called it *El Día del Pavo.* She said that it was the day you eat turkey, but I always thought, what does a turkey have to do with a holiday or why is a holiday called such a thing? I didn't understand back then.

◆

November 2000

My dad is in the kitchen busy with the turkey. This time he wanted to make sure that we have something to eat, so he bought the turkey two days ago. He finds the recipes to make the meal, but he ends up cooking what I call my dad's own style of dinner. No sweet potatoes, but creamed baked potatoes. No yam and cranberry sauce, but squash stuffed with *chorizo.* No pumpkin pie, but apple pie, and something that we can't miss—*chile.* It is the hot, homemade salsa that makes anybody's stomach burn if they are not used to it. My mom prepares the salsa by grilling the chile and the tomatoes. Even the smell awakens my senses, bringing alive memories of my mom cooking while we were still living in Mexico. We sit at the table and without praying we start eating. We are hungry, and we are happy that we have a new holiday to celebrate together.

◆

I remember it was hard for me—this process of acculturation—when I first moved to the United States four years ago. I wanted to celebrate *El Día de la Independencia*, but I realized that here Americans did it on July 4th and not on September 16th. Surprisingly, Americans celebrated Cinco de Mayo, while in Mexico it is not a recognized holiday. Not only was it difficult becoming accustomed to new traditions, but to a different language.

During my first year in Houston, I wanted to keep reading and writing in Spanish because I was afraid of not making it in a foreign country in which the official language was not my native tongue. I was embarrassed to speak my broken sentences or make a mistake. At the time, I was taking English lessons, and a teacher sensed my alienation. She said something that still comes back to my mind when I feel out of place. "There is a poet who said that your home is not where you come from, but where you go to." I was offended, since my mind was full of ethnocentric thoughts. Later, I understood it and took it as advice.

I was surprised this last September when I forgot *El Día de la Independencia*. I guess the reason was the distance of a celebration going on in my country, especially in La Plaza of my *pueblito* where paper decorations highlight the colors of the Mexican flag. Later, I felt guilty for not remembering this day. For a moment I thought that I was there within the crowd of people listening to the fireworks and watching the kids screaming and running away from the *buscapies*, the explosive and shining firecrackers that may follow your feet—especially if you try to avoid them. I was enjoying the smell of *elotes*, the delicious corn on the cob topped with sour cream and cheese, and the *churros*, the fried and sugared bread. I was looking at the noisy salesman making an effort to gather people at the Tupperware auction in his bright yellow stand. An unintentional rhythmic melody was filling the air with all the people's talk and laughter, waiting for the coming event at midnight. It came and I was there. I was listening to the people excitedly crying out the names of the independence heroes.

Now I'm happy that I not only have *El Día de la Independencia* or *El Día de los Muertos* to celebrate, but Thanksgiving too. On this day I am thankful for having a new home just like the Pilgrims were many years ago.

Independence Battle

I HAVE THREE BROTHERS: two older ones, Gerardo and Martín, and one younger than me, Andrés. I always envied their freedom to go and do whatever they wanted. According to my mom, only the men are allowed to do that. My brothers became strong and independent, and I, the only girl, had to stay home and watch them come and go as they pleased. In fact, there was a point in my life when I hated to be a woman. I was probably around twelve, but at that age I sure felt old enough to make my own decisions. I hated staying home and having my parents or brothers as chaperones every time I wanted to go out. Even though more than once I resented my brothers for their freedom, I realize now that they belong to a big part of the puzzle of my life.

Gerardo, the oldest, moved out of the house to go to the university in Guadalajara at the age of eighteen. I wanted to move out and be like him. I couldn't wait to finish high school and go to the university. The small town we lived in didn't have a university, so I knew that I had to move to the city in order to keep studying. This was my dream—the dream of having my own apartment and my own free time to do whatever I wanted. But my dad woke me up from that dream.

"I'm moving to Guadalajara to study over there," I innocently said when I was about sixteen years old.

"If you go there, your mom will have to go live with you," my dad said.

That was cold water thrown on my face. After that, the idea was buried, no longer appealing to me. I never brought up the subject again.

Instead, right after high school I came to Houston to live. I lived in my uncle's house for a few months, in which I had a little more freedom, but it didn't last long. After less than a year, my family came to stay here too.

Gerardo never came back to live with us. He stayed in Mexico. Now at the age of thirty I don't think there is a possibility that he will ever come back to live with us again. I think he likes his loneliness and the fact that he doesn't have to hear my mom's insisting request to clean his place. "Gerardo, you should be ashamed of yourself! How can you live like this?" This time I agree with her. The smell of trash piled up in one corner for several weeks and the rotten food sitting on the table bathing in the hot summer weather of Los Cabos is not very appealing. Gerardo doesn't pay attention to my mother's complaints. He has a great sense of humor. In fact, I had never seen him down until two summers ago when our conversation turned to the subject of relationships.

"I can't find a girlfriend because I'm ugly, right?"

I nodded. The truth is that he is not a great looking guy. He went bald in his early twenties, and I think his braces didn't help much either, but I let him know that I thought he would find a good girl. Inside me though, my heart crashed and I begged that God would hear my prayers to help him find someone.

Martín is my second oldest brother. He has cooked for us as long as I can remember, but I think he just does it because he likes eating a lot and not because he enjoys cooking. He has never been fat though, until now that he is married. How Martín finished his accounting degree I don't know because I hardly saw him grab a book to study. Everyday he went to "school," came home to eat and sleep, and went out with his friends. I hated him. I hated the fact that he was never responsible and that he would go out all the time. In addition to this, he was the one who convinced my mom not to let me go out anywhere. "He is a man and you are a woman," my mom would defend him. That phrase stuck in my mind, and dead mice fall out of my stomach when I hear it. However, I would forget my hatred when time for breakfast came and he cooked *chilaquiles*. I waited in the kitchen while he fried the tortillas in tomato sauce, later adding the cheese and the sour cream. When we came to live in Houston four years ago, Martín stayed in Mexico. His deep roots didn't allow him to move anywhere away from his little town. Martín is twenty-eight and a different person now. His marriage and his little baby boy, David, have changed him. He has become a responsible man, and I sure don't hate him anymore. I still miss his *chilaquiles*.

My youngest brother, Andrés, is my mom's spoiled one. He was one of my best friends when we were growing up. I used to make him play Barbie dolls with me when we were kids. He is now twenty-two and has turned into a good-looking guy. There was a point when he got good grades, but that was in high school before he started dating. I guess we grew apart when I realized he was no longer my confidant but his way out when he needed a favor. Now his full-time job, his red sports car, and his sleazy girlfriend are more important than school.

Andrés' girlfriend stayed overnight one night, and then another night, turning into weeks, and now it's been months. I was surprised at the beginning that my mom—as conservative as she is—would allow this to happen, but she never said anything strong enough to stop it.

"He's in a serious relationship now," she said once.

I just gave her a fake smile, thinking how silly that sounded.

I'm convinced that I don't want to have the same liberty that my brother has, but at least I'd like my mom to be more reasonable about my relationships. I'm not allowed to hold hands with my boyfriend in the same room with my mom. Complaining is out of the question. My mom has always celebrated that Andrés has had too many girlfriends, but she would never do the same thing with me because I'm a "woman." Not only that, but she has implied that my job is to be trained for marriage, and that includes cooking, in case I marry a "macho" man. I think that is the reason I don't get along with the kitchen.

My mom has done a good job of making me realize that the only option I have to get out of the house is marriage. She also made me realize that I don't have the same privileges that my brothers had.

A friend once told me something that really stuck in my mind: "Spend all the time you can with your parents now because in the future they might not be with you. Then you'll miss them." At that moment I agreed with her, but I don't know if I feel the same way anymore. Maybe I'm not ready to be independent yet, but I know that someday I will be. Then I will have my dream come true. I will have my own place and cook if I want to or not cook at all. I will watch television late and have a plant that I'll probably kill. I'll clean my bedroom when I feel like it. Or not.

mission to smoke

IT WAS ALMOST SIX O'CLOCK ON ONE OF THOSE OPPRESSIVE, hot Houston afternoons, and I was waiting in my car for my dad to get out of work. Suddenly, the clanging sound of my dad's keys as he opened the door startled me. It took me by surprise as I had forgotten for a moment that I was waiting for him. I had always thought of my dad as a superhero, someone that could do no wrong, almost saintly. Just before he got in the car, memories of my dad always having the answers to all of my questions had started coming to me.

I remembered his coming home every day with his brown suit like a very important and dedicated person. I remembered him cooking us sugar crêpes at six in the morning every day before my brother and I went to school. This superhero image fell from the sky as he closed the door and the little air space was filled with that cigarette smell that knocked me down like a cartoon character crashed by a bus. At that moment I imagined that my little car was no longer blue, but gray with black spots all over the outside. I wanted to say something to him. I wanted to let him know that he is too old to be smoking, and I wanted to know how long he had been hiding from us the fact that he smokes. I couldn't. I rolled my window down so I could give my lungs some clean air, if you can call Houston's air "clean." Instead of telling him what was on my mind, I just said, "How was your day?" and kept on driving.

A few months before this incident, my brother told me that he thought he had seen my dad's car on the road and the driver was holding a cigarette. He didn't see the driver's face, but he was sure it was the same black Pontiac my dad drives. "My dad would never do that," I thought. We argued, but he was so sure that it seemed almost possible. I felt disappointed but not fully convinced of my brother's words. Now it all made sense. I knew that he had been right.

Now my dad's habit is obvious to me despite the fact that he tries to do everything he can to cover it up. On the weekends, he will say that he has to run to the store because he forgot to buy milk or something, when in reality he goes on his "mission to smoke." Sometimes when he says he's working in the backyard, I've noticed how he disappears for long periods of time. Again, he's on his secret mission to smoke. This "teenage-like" attitude of trying to hide his actions comes along when we are watching television and a commercial comes on about teaching your kids not to smoke. He tries to change the channel or leave the room.

I have never seen my dad smoking and I don't think I ever want to even hear about it. I'm not even sure if my mom knows about his smoking. I do remember that once after my dad was back from one of those missions, my mom caught the smell and she directly asked, "Andrés, do you smoke?"

"No! How could you believe that?"

I thought, "It's almost impossible that anyone would believe such a lie." My dad should have known that everyone was aware of what smoke smells like—even my mom. I ran into my room because I didn't want to hear the rest of the conversation. From my understanding, he made her believe that he wasn't smoking, and yes, my mom is naive enough to believe him.

The last and most recent incident that brought the truth to the surface was the day of my dad's recent surgery. While my mom and I were sitting beside his bed, a nurse came to fill out a questionnaire in which he had to confess that he smoked only "a little bit." I know his words were pulled out against his will, but he couldn't lie to the nurse even though I was standing there. He never turned to look at me.

Still, after that incident nothing has changed. My dad's smoking habit is something that we definitively don't talk about, and I don't know if we ever will. His "missions to smoke" are still a secret to most of my family, even though they are no longer to me. I'm sure he is too embarrassed to stain his impeccable figure among his family, so I try to understand him.

I'm not a kid anymore and many things have changed since I was a kid, but my love for my father remains the same. Even superheroes make mistakes.

Padre . . .	Father . . .
Tú eres como un niño	You are my loyal companion
que me acompaña	who lends me his hand
en mi camino,	in my long journey through life,
sonriendo y queriéndome	smiling and loving me
como el amor puro	like the simple love to which
de un suspiro.	the air is joined to a sigh.

inherited images
Aisha Calderon

THE CALENDAR WAS MOVING QUITE RAPIDLY and yet my dad's promise was still unmet. Days melted into weeks, then months, and still nothing. I was trying to establish ownership of his tucked-away object, one I had been coveting for years, but which needed to be repaired. My repeated attempts at reminding him of this usually went something to the tune of, "Dad, you said you would have it fixed by now!" To which he replied, standard for all my wants, "Have some patience, Aisha." Patience, I thought, I've been waiting years, and, besides that, my creative juices were flowing. Quelling them was not an option.

Shiny metallic hardware sheltered its sides, while black plastic parts made up the rectangular middle portion. The lens was round and firm with numbers and meanings that I didn't understand yet. As my fingers wrapped around it, I could feel the heavy hand I would be dealt if I broke it. The clicking sound it emitted was so crisp and professional that every time I would sneak into his closet to see it, I pictured the previous possessor on safari, high above an old VW bug taking pictures of cheetahs for *National Geographic*, or some fabulous man snapping shots of Twiggy in London. The smell that lingered in the tattered case reminded me of something slowly fermenting in my grandfather's house, kind of damp, not unpleasant like mildew, just distant like it came from a far-off time when I wasn't in existence.

This perfect time-capturer was purchased when my dad came to L.A. from Nicaragua. Being an appreciator of photography, and having newly acquired fatherly instincts, he wanted to celebrate our every step and, therefore, had to buy a camera. Thinking that finances would prevent him from attaining a quality one, he was happily considering a cheap, mass-produced point-and-shoot. One day, while perusing the classifieds, he came across an ad that read, "Nikon FE, like new, comes with strap and case, $350." He said initially he thought it was a misprint, but after making the phone call and confirming the deal, he knew he had scored. Then, after years of tirelessly immortalizing his children standing in front of somewhere proudly portraying my brother's buckteeth and my glowing red Afro along with our enduring Fonzie thumb-extended pose, my dad put the Nikon away. Perhaps this neglect made the shutter stick, so by the time my interest in the art surfaced, the camera needed some serious mending.

My love for the craft occurred during two different times in my life. The first was the foundation for what would later become a real full-blown passion. When I was a little whippersnapper, during the ages of five to ten, I remember going over to Mamacita's house, my mom's mom, and being intensely engaged with all the pictures she had meticulously nailed to the wall. I used to stare for hours at ancestral faces that looked regal and unfamiliar. I would mentally transport myself to that day in the picture just by obsessively fixating myself on their surroundings and closing my eyes to envision the still. It was like magic. Sometimes I would call Mamacita over and have her explain with great detail everybody in the shot. I wanted to know exactly who took the picture and what was going on the day of the shoot. *"¿Quién es él, Mamacita?"* I would inquire in our native tongue. *"Ése era mi hermano Manuel José, él se murió cuando yo era muy joven."* Usually during this phase of memory lane, as she went through the line-up of our kin, I would notice a pensive state taking over her eyes and heart. She would momentarily crumble into these pictures and let out a guttural *"Aaaahhh, cómo es la vida."* I knew she was sad because these people no longer walked among us, but at the same time I was extremely grateful for the reliving of those moments through this medium.

Later, as I grew into my own skin and entered high school, I developed a deeper love and understanding for the technique. This is when I pleaded with my dad to hand over my inheritance, so I too could continue the traditions started by generations before me. Plus, since I didn't have any competition from my brother, who had been bequeathed my mother's musical talent as his artistic means, I knew the camera was perfect for me. Given that the shutter on the Nikon had to be replaced, which, of course, meant lots of money and therefore a long wait, I resorted to purchasing a point-and-shoot Pentax for the reasonably low price of $39.99. Obviously, it didn't compare to my dad's old-school gem, but for the time being, it would have to do. During these years I became the vital historian present in every group of friends, always taking pictures, but never in them. I seemed to have a knack for perfectly capturing Fred's laugh-out-loud goofy faces or Jorge's consistently perverted grins, while even the occasional candid shot of someone just waking up got recognized as picturesque. Soon my photographs were being duplicated two and three times over. "Could I borrow the negatives to make doubles?" became a customary response after the first viewing of my pictures.

From then on, I became completely fascinated and largely perplexed by the whole process. With just the right amount of chemicals and light, these awesome pieces of paper could be manipulated to transcend the bounds of life. "It's like time travel," I used to think. It was also during this time I started linking my affinity for the craft with my morbid obsession with death. I associated the taking of a picture to be reminiscent of death, because for me it seemed like the murdering of the moment. In order to selfishly retain that piece of time forever, I had to kill it. And I liked the idea of controlling and timing death, so it became my weird connotation for my hobby. All the same, I sailed on the waves of continuous experimenting.

Aisha Calderon

Finally, after years of inquiry and constant pestering, during my last year of high school, just in time for my non-college departure, my dad brought me a freshened-up camera bag complete with a longer strap, newly purchased attachments, and, nestled deep inside, the just-operated-on Nikon FE. Smiling from ear to ear, I reached for the bag and, like a Christmas present, tore open the receptacle it came in and lifted the camera out. The skies opened, music played, and stars twinkled. "So cool. Thanks, Dad!" This time, rightfully holding the vessel of art, I immediately aimed it at my dad. Through the lens I could see his dark, indigenous features appreciating his only daughter's happiness. I firmly pressed on the silver button and froze that moment forever.

Mining My Hills
Melissa Cantor

THE ANCIENT MINING TOWN WHERE I WAS BORN is not cold or gray or haunted, but thriving and hot. To the Mayans who originally populated my city, its name, Tegucigalpa, meant "silver hills." Aside from the inescapable annual school trips to El Mochito, I never saw much of these eponymous silver mines. But I definitely saw enough of the hills. I hated them. I hated that all the cars in Tegucigalpa are stick shifts because people think automatic cars won't make it up steep cliffs. Ricardo's car was a stick, and half the time it never made it up the incline to my house, anyway. Needless to say, my hatred for the hills was most acute when at 3 a.m., weary and nauseous after a night of drinking and dancing, I found myself climbing one, dragging my black heels behind me by the straps, while my boyfriend cursed his useless stick-shift VW for the fourth night in a row.

I also hated the hills because they mandate vertical architecture. All the houses in Tegucigalpa are split-level because it's impossible to buy a wide, flat piece of land. That means that on these nights, when I finally made it up the incline and through my gate, I had to then crawl up two flights of stairs before finding solace from the terrain on the blissfully flat topography of my bed. My uncle owns a construction company, and he built the marble-tiled staircase I labored up those nights. He's designed hundreds of split-levels and is a self-proclaimed expert on building on cliffs. I hated the hills because they give him something to brag about, because I can see his bearded chin rising defiantly as he turns his mouth into a sneer and claims he can build on anything, anywhere.

I hated the hills because they prolong the sound of the ice-cream man. In Tegucigalpa, penniless men push freezers up 80-degree angles under a tropical noon sun, all in the hopes of selling a four-Lempira icicle to a wealthy family craving dessert. One afternoon at 2:22 p.m., I bought an ice-cream sandwich from one of these men. For the next few months, at precisely 2:22 in the afternoon, Ezequiel rang my doorbell, and I sampled every possible flavor of frozen dairy. Eventually, I consumed too many kiwi- and mango-flavored *paletas* to still care about how many children Ezequiel had to feed. I hated the hills because long before the doorbell pierced my comfort, they trapped the two-o'clock echo of poverty and inequality and carried it to my window in the form of the ring-ring of the bell on his ice-cream cart.

I hated the hills and the accompanying sense of claustrophobia until I moved away. But now that I live in a city where horizons stretch out flat and forever, like stale futures, I miss the shade the hills gave me. I feel vulnerable and exposed on the smooth expanses of South Florida where everything is visible from miles away. I miss streets where you can only see three cars ahead of you before the whole road curves and then you can't count the number of cars slowing your progress. I miss mountains that stand between you and the sky, so even though you can feel it, you can't really see the sun that gnaws at your skin.

I miss how sheltered I was in my tiny city, where everything is fifteen minutes from my parents and the friends I've had my whole life. I was safe in the hills because they shielded me from expectations and temptations. There is nothing I want to accomplish in Tegucigalpa, because I've either done it already or know I never will. I can't fail at writing because there is no such thing as a writer in the commerce-driven Third World. I can't disappoint my family in Tegus because the hills draw impenetrable barriers between social classes, and I would never face the danger of falling in love with a man my parents would disapprove of. In Tegucigalpa, I would get engaged to a young entrepreneur and never give my heart away to a saxophone player I can't take home. "Can't he afford a haircut?" they would say, if they ever met John. "Do you want to be forty years old and spending every night in the back room of a country western bar?" In Tegucigalpa I can mess up and it's okay, because nothing is at stake.

I feel like I should not, but I miss the comfort and the ease of life there. The danger of that mountainous terrain is my safety blanket, and those hills are my haven. The house whispers of Spanish and *merengue*, the taste of pinto beans and *nacatamales,* memories of my youth, its freedom and irresponsibility. When I venture back into these silver hills, no one can see where I've gone because of the curves of the winding streets. But when I walk the flat roads of America, people can watch me go, trace my path, and witness the inevitable stumble.

Mutts

Adam Castañeda

I REMEMBER THOSE DEFORMED PUPPIES like they had been born yesterday. I can see a dozen balls of mangled fur squirming over each other, desperate to reach the nipple deprived by their mother. She just looks at them, her big brown eyes horrified at the monstrosities she has brought into this world: a box of live mini-canine Frankensteins. Some do not have the right number of limbs. Some do, but the length of their limbs don't match. Others have gross scabs over their knees, large caps of gray, hairless skin. Others still have a misty glaze in the eyes, as if someone slapped Vaseline over their infant faces. All are dripping colorful liquid from their noses. Imagine that gruesome sight times two. Two litters of deformed puppies, each one in their own box on opposite ends of the yard, yearning for some source of nourishment and affection. Their mothers didn't give it to them and neither did I or any other member of our family. I was eight years old, and I remember thinking that I had seen these sick puppies before—in a nightmare.

Our attention was drawn to another box, a third litter of puppies, these born intact and healthy. There were six of them. Five had already finished suckling, and the sixth one, the one we almost adopted, was checking each of his mother's teats to see if there was anything left over. He wasn't the runt of the litter; he was just a little glutton. He had only been born a few days before, but he already sported a thick coat of fur, the most attractive combination of browns and blacks, that made him look like an expensive snow seal plush doll.

My father made sure this group of puppies was well taken care of. They were housed in a sturdy box with a few blankets for warmth and comfort. My grandmother made sure that if the mother ran out of milk, there was always a bowl of the store-bought kind or water to keep their little stomachs full and their mouths moist.

Three litters of puppies were born on our property during a two-week period. If my family were the type of people who constantly looked for attention, then this event would have been viewed as a neighborhood miracle and, maybe, even gone down in urban legend history. But that didn't happen. No one knew about the batch of heavenly puppies and their monster counterparts. Everything was kept pretty hush-hush.

Our neighborhood was located in the heart of Houston. Surrounded by freeways on each side, Lindale Park was a haven for strays and middle-class rejects from the Heights. At the time, property in the neighborhood wasn't worth much, so the whites weren't interested in buying empty lots and building handsome brick houses. It was just Hispanics, neither rich nor poor, white or Mexican, here or there. And everyone seemed to have a mutt.

The dog responsible for this family scandal was our very own German shepherd/Chow mix mutt, Aladdin. We never envisioned Aladdin as a pimp, but here he was, a father three times over. We had noticed that he had been dreadfully busy these last few months, creeping out of the gate each night and returning with his black coat soiled in dirt and mulch. One of the three lucky dames was Elsa, the full-blooded Chow from next door who had the swagger and mannerisms of a Montrose hooker. The other two were both mutts, like Aladdin. Those two were the ones who bore the deformed litters. One was a hound dog of indeterminable breed, the other was a coffee-colored stray whose long history of miscegenation had erased any distinct physical traits.

For the next couple of days, my brother and I tried our best to nurture the desirable puppies. We knew that we would have to sell them. So, when the time came, we were well prepared.

We didn't cry or complain. Our only demand was to keep the chubby snow seal. My parents agreed to this plea bargain, and we played with him in the grass. I couldn't help but glance over at the box containing his brothers and sisters. They would be traded for five dollars, no questions asked. Inside, I felt that what was going on was wrong, and not just selling the puppies, whose mother was tied up behind the garage so she couldn't protect her young, but the way the deformed ones were being neglected as well.

Surprisingly, there were no takers for the "good" puppies. I let myself have a sigh of relief. The puppies would stay with their mother and father, and now maybe we could start caring for the little monsters too.

I went to school that Monday. When I came back, the only four-legged creature in the vicinity was Aladdin, lounging in a bed of mulch scratching at the back of his neck, a habit that eventually would reveal a case of fleas and would, ultimately, lead to his death. I looked for the puppies, but I couldn't find them. My grandmother noticed I was poking around the garage, and then she told me. She had called the pound earlier that day to take away the diseased animals and their mothers too. The good litter had been taken away with the bad. They were probably all dead that very moment. "We don't need fleas *con tanto perro*," my grandmother said.

◆

The SPCA had always freaked me out. In every cage was an animal made docile by drugs, patronizing petting, and unwanted baths. I hated the way the dogs looked at you with their big, wet eyes when you passed their cell, their heads slowly following your movement across the hall. If for some reason they caught your fancy, they'd whimper until you came back. If you ignored them and walked off to another section of the sterile building, they'd stop and prepare their sad faces for someone else.

My mother always said that we weren't dog people. As a child, she never had one. Her mother always thought they were nuisances. They could barely afford to feed themselves, much less a mangy dog. In later years, Grandpa and Grandma would become dependent on having dogs in their presence. After their houseful of children emptied out, they needed something to replace the noise, and the barking of a dog seemed like the perfect fit. Dogs seemed to die at an alarming rate at their house too, so mom's youngest sister decided to put an end to pet-keeping at my grandparents' house when Oreo, a cuddly toy breed that looked like a rug, ran out of the front gate and got smashed by their neighbor's car pulling out of their driveway.

Still, Mom thought it was only fitting for my youngest brother to have a puppy, just so he couldn't say later in life that he was deprived of this quintessential American must-have and rite of passage.

What rattled my nerves even more was going to the SPCA—part kennel, part dumping ground for adult dogs who weren't wanted. It was here where Aladdin had spent the remaining days of his life, itching at the fleas that cut bloody welts into his skin. That place was an asylum. From the moment the door was opened, every dog on the cement lane hurled themselves at their cage doors, barking as if that moment was their last moment to do so. We didn't spend much time in there, except I will never forgot the tallest dog I've ever seen, one of those handsome grays that come out on Sesame Street, a good five feet tall.

As we were heading out, we got sight of a woman entering the little dog dormitory with a small terrier in her arms. I fell in love with her at first sight—the dog that is. We learned from the woman that the dog was indeed a she, close to two years old, a terrier mix, not purebred, and had such a congenial personality that she was being used as a companion for the lonely elderly.

"We could definitely stand to part with her if we knew she was going to a good home," she said, sizing up my disheveled family, five anxious and nerve-rattled individuals ready to make a hasty decision and hightail it out of there.

We were introduced to the terrier immediately. We were allotted a private room where we could observe how she interacted when the staff was not around. It was obvious that she was a house dog who was fully trained in the ways of civilized bathroom manners. "We'll take her," my father said after five minutes.

"About time," my brother said.

As I held Ashes, the name I had christened her, in my arms, I realized with much sadness that we weren't going to do her any good. Every pet I had, had ended up dead. I knew that she wouldn't be with us for more than two years, and my predictions would eventually prove correct. That day I felt like I was helping to make another batch of deformed puppies, even though I was holding the perfect specimen of a child's playmate.

The sanchez sisters go to san Antonio

MOM AND HER SISTER, Aunt Michelle, had been planning a three-day getaway to San Antonio for weeks. It was pretty exciting. Not that San Antonio was special for us, but this time, the women were leaving the men behind. Very big deal. The idea sounded good over the phone, but putting it into action was another matter. Aunt Angie worked, so there was difficulty trying to accommodate her schedule. Aunt Blanca was cheap, so there was difficulty trying to devise a way to fit her whole clan in our hotel rooms. Now, none of this set very well with Mom. She's pretty by-the-book. She doesn't like to hear about extenuating circumstances, especially since she's the type of person who bears hers silently. "If they really want to go, they'll go. It's not like Angie can't call in sick for a day, and Blanca needs to quit being a cheapskate." So the whole thing ended up being Aunt Michelle, her two kids, Laila and Ricky, Grandma and cousin Amanda, Mom, myself, and my two younger brothers in a two-car caravan.

The whole thing was doomed before we even left Houston.

Aunt Michelle was thirty minutes late getting to our house. She was supposed to pick up Grandma and Amanda and then drop them off at our house so they could ride with us. Mom was already a little aggravated since Michelle had waited until the last minute the night before to get the ice chest ready and the stroller prepared. Mom was up until midnight because of that, and that's never a good thing. The morning was pretty uneventful after that, except for the fact that my brother had to take over driving for Michelle because she was about to pass out from sleepiness.

We had left Houston at around seven in the morning. We left early because we hoped to spend the whole first day at Fiesta Texas. My brother Aaron, Amanda, and I were eagerly awaiting the roller coasters because the ones in Astroworld sucked. It was soon apparent that we weren't going to meet our deadline of getting to the park right when it opened. Mom had a line etched across her forehead. After a lot of driving around, we finally found our hotel, a very nice and economical Holiday Inn. It was located close to the River Walk, right in the center of downtown San Antonio. It was nice to relax in our rooms, breathing the scent of new furniture. All the beds and sofas and chairs seemed oversized, like they were built to engulf you in comfort. My family stayed in one room, while Aunt Michelle and the rest of the gang stayed in a room directly across the hall.

We heard a knock on the door and no sooner had we opened it than in spilled Michelle, breathless. "I forgot the season passes," she heaved. Mom didn't say anything. She just turned around and continued unpacking, but I could tell by her knotted hands and pursed lips that she was trembling inside. "And I can't find the kids' swim stuff. I'm gonna have to run to Wal-Mart."

"What?"

It was on.

"Michelle, that's why we left early, so we could get in the park at ten. It's past noon and we're still in the hotel."

"Well, I'm sorry! I get nervous traveling with you because you're such a control freak and such a timekeeper. My God, no one's going to die because we get to Fiesta Texas late."

"So what are we going to do? *We* are going to be stuck waiting for you!"

"Just go without me, then. I'll catch up later. Besides, Mom needs to go to Wal-Mart too." This was strange, considering Grandma wouldn't have said she wanted to go to Wal-Mart if Michelle hadn't left everything behind. Grandma was going just so Michelle wouldn't be left with the two small kids. We all knew it.

In the car, Mom was sweating around her lips and forehead. Mom never sweats because of heat. She sweats because of an emotion, usually exasperation. Her cell phone began to ring in her purse and she swerved slightly trying to reach it. It was Michelle. "Hey, listen. I forgot the stroller in your car. I'm going to need it when I get to Fiesta Texas." Mom didn't even wait for her to finish. She slammed the cell phone shut and threw it back in her purse. "I can't believe her!" She didn't say anything else and neither did any of us. If we were hungry, thirsty, or needed to go to the bathroom, we didn't show it. We just sat there, our hands in our laps, pretending we didn't know what was going on and hoping we would go unnoticed.

She dropped my brothers and Amanda off at the front of the park gate. She had to stay behind with the stroller until Michelle came. The three of us trotted off in search of thrills, spills, and screams, but soon the heat put an end to our merriment. The theme park had been built in the middle of an orange canyon. The sun reflected off the walls of the rocks and created a bowl of simmering heat. We remained pretty melancholy for hours to come. The pleasure was gone because we knew something was going wrong.

"So what should we get on next, guys?" Amanda asked, even though she didn't appear to be amused by anything in particular. Thirteen years old, Amanda was ready to live like a teenager, but here she was, stuck in a lame theme park, her hands on her hips, waiting for her "cool" older cousins to do something grown-up.

"Let's try the Rattler," my brother offered. At the mention of the name, my stomach churned. The Rattler just happened to be the ride I was hoping to avoid. Tall, rough, and Texan, the wooden roller coaster was a force to be reckoned with. Aside from a hefty drop and two spiraling towers of nonstop circular motion, the Rattler was extremely uncomfortable, the ancient wood creaking and swaying as if it were an aged, arthritic old man.

I hid my apprehension, and we began the ascent. It seemed like forever before we reached the last upward ramp. By then, I was actually excited about the upcoming thrill. Peeking over the wooden barricade that separated the line from the cart platform, even more good news. The line was short. It was all good. Then, in a manifestation of negative energy, in an allegory of our cursed trip, in a trick of irony, we saw the sign: "Closed for repair." Drenched in sweat, I was too exasperated to complain. We trudged back down the eternity from which we had come and resigned ourselves to Superman Escape and a host of assorted kiddy rides.

At about lunchtime we made our way back to the park entrance. We searched out Mom, Michelle, and the cooler we knew they would bring. We found all three of them along with Grandma at the far corner of the picnic area. Laila and Ricky were still in their twin stroller, irritated by the heat. They swatted at themselves, their uncoordinated movements made even more awkward and sluggish by the lack of moisture in their bodies. The three of us slid onto the wooden benches and waited to be told what to do. It wasn't that we didn't know how to make sandwiches, but we didn't want to make a false move that would ignite a stick of dynamite.

Michelle approached us from the parking lot, carrying bags of snacks. Mom, unpacking the cooler, didn't say anything until she saw the bags. The wick had been lighted.

Adam Castañeda

"Michelle, did you really need to bring three bags of groceries? We're just having sandwiches."

"Hello, what are we going to eat on? We need napkins and forks."

"For sandwiches?"

"Mom, I'm thirsty."

"Hold on, Laila."

"Guys, the stuff's on the table. Y'all can make your own sandwiches."

"Michelle, what's all this?"

"Mayonnaise. Do you got a problem? I like mayonnaise."

"What happened to keeping things simple?"

"What's complicated? My God. We need Coke. We need chips. We need . . ."

"We need crackers and Cheese Whiz? This is just supposed to hold us over until dinner."

"Hold yourself over. I'm chowing down."

"So you're on a diet now, or what?"

"Michelle, don't mess with me right now."

"I said what's wrong? Why aren't you eating?"

"I'm not hungry."

"Why are you looking like you lost your best friend?"

"Believe me, I didn't lose my best friend."

Michelle just looked at Mom. Was she really being this difficult? This mean? Had they both just spent what little money they had saved for a weekend away from stressful lives, only to find the negative in each other? If this were a play, I could imagine someone in the audience letting out an obnoxious "Duh." The realization was too much for Michelle. In an instant, her lips were quivering, she was standing, and she was stuffing her food into bags, making sure the mayonnaise was coming with her.

"I can't believe you're so stupid," she told my mother, her voice shrill and tight. "Yelling in front of all these people. You're so dumb," she said, her own voice rising, drawing the attention of the families around us, their white faces looking up from their white bread sandwiches to look at these two crazy women who were not white. Mom tried to stop her, doing her best to console without apologizing, but she failed miserably. The next thing I remember is Michelle driving off with Laila and Ricky peering out the window at us, their faces wondering why their lunch had been interrupted.

Grandma sat down and sighed. Her red hair had darkened with perspiration and was pasted to her forehead. Her flip-flops dangled from her feet, barely touching the ground. She seemed tired, fatigued despite her stoutness and good health. She shook her head and said, "I just don't know what has happened to these girls. They get married and I lose control. I just don't know." Then we all started crying. Not real crying, but silent-tears crying. We shed them for Mom, Aunt Michelle, our spoiled meal, and a vacation that was over before it even started.

starving for perfection
Dalia Cruz

"I JUST DON'T GET IT, what is it that these girls see in the mirror? How can they look at themselves and call themselves fat? Is there something lacking in their brain, some type of chemical imbalance that leads them to have a distorted image of their bodies?"

I can still recall with such clarity the emotions that were provoked in me as my eleventh-grade classmate posed the above questions. At that point in time, I promise I wanted to turn around and slap her across the face! It would have taken a lot of courage on my part to carry out these violent desires, however. As a matter of fact, it took a lot to build up the strength to finally turn and face my accuser. As I slowly paired up the monstrosity of her comments to her face, I could see her eyes looking fiercely at me as she moved her thick lips to slowly torture me with every word that came out of her mouth. How dare she express herself in such a careless manner over a topic that filled me with so many complexities? How dare she categorize me as mentally ill? What did she know about the day-to-day hurdles that I had to jump in order to reach my state of perfection?

But, of course, she didn't understand. She was just like everyone else, just like my parents, my brothers, the rest of my other family members, friends, coworkers, therapist, etc. No one seemed to understand the fear that had been tormenting me for the past months. Well, I guess one person did. Her name was Ana.

Ana was my new best friend who I had encountered my junior year of high school. For the past three years I had been extremely happy growing up in the "bubble" that I found myself in—surrounded by students who shared the same interests as I did. We worked diligently on schoolwork and were competitive when it came to practicing our sports. My coaches, both in and out of school, always emphasized the importance of maintaining a healthy appearance. Just when the pressures of living up to these high standards became extremely hectic, however, I found Ana. Ana understood exactly what I was going through; in fact it was Ana who gave me the strength I needed to pursue my ideal state of perfection. I was no longer content with a flat stomach and a lean body. I wanted more than that. I wanted my bones to outline the garments that clothed my massive body; I became obsessed with turning my body into a canvas.

My teacher continued with her lecture on eating disorders. "Let me warn you, class, that the images you're about to see may be a little disturbing." As my classmates grimaced in awe at the photos of young women with emaciated bodies, I wasn't as disturbed as they were. "Wow," I remember thinking, "I admire the strength that these girls have. It takes a lot of self-control to reach a body that is fat free." Apparently, my perspective of beauty was considered "unhealthy" by the rest of the world. As my teacher continued, I noticed that just like the women in these pictures, I had also developed an intense fear of becoming FAT. I felt angry and ashamed of my self-destruction. However, Ana was already stronger than I was. I was not ready to stop, not just yet.

"Hey Dalia, I noticed that you have gained a little weight. You're not as thin as you used to be. You look better now," Carmen, a coworker of mine, would often tell me. I was aware that I no longer could fit into my size 1 jeans. In fact, size 3 was beginning to fit me a bit snug. Lately, I had been training with weights since my high school coaches often encouraged this in order to build stronger muscles. Needless to say, the added weight training to my already rigorous workouts was increasing my appetite and I was eating a lot more than I had been accustomed to. I could see that my body was slowly changing, and, at first, I was somewhat satisfied with the results.

"Wow," my aunts would say as they admired my evolving curves, "you actually have a butt and hips now. You're looking a lot healthier. You know that Latin men like women with a little meat." How I detested the way in which their chubby cheeks inflated like balloons as they smiled and applauded my new body.

As I began to see that the numbers on the scale were gradually increasing and that now I had to shop for size 5 jeans, the word "healthy" began to take on a negative connotation. For me, healthy meant chubby, fuller, grotesquely fat. I remember the countless hours that I spent looking at pictures of thin models; their skeletal frames obviously did not show the signs of soft roundness in which my "healthy" body had now been disguised. I didn't care much for this "healthy" appearance that my relatives had labeled me as, or for my often-complimented, pretty, sweet, round-shaped face. I came to detest these features that belonged to me because, in the world of perfectly thin supermodels, neither roundness nor a healthy appearance were acceptable. I was not concerned about enhancing the beauty that others found in my face. Instead, I was obsessed with reaching that gaunt, lanky figure that all the models I turned to for inspiration had. What did I care of the painted picture that Latin men had of their ideal woman? I had my own idea of what beauty was, and it was I who had to be satisfied with my physical appearance. It did not matter how often I was reminded of my pretty smile or my good personality, it was the numbers on the scale that determined my beauty—nothing else.

There was no way that I was going to allow myself to get any fatter. I felt the need to take control. I was by no means content with the image that stared back at me when I stood in front of a mirror. Therefore, I began adhering to a lifestyle that required a strict caloric intake and a tough exercise regime. My days were measured in calories, I began by only consuming

1000 calories per day but that number drastically went down to 500 and then 300.

"I had an excellent day today," I would often tell my oblivious friends, "I ended my day at a negative caloric intake." It seems that the more I pushed myself, the more I demanded. I was in competition with my own self. Ana helped me achieve many victories, which encouraged me to continue with her by my side. Being able to lose four pounds in five days was amazing because after all, nothing tasted as good as being thin did.

My rapid weight loss, however, soon began to concern those who surrounded me. As my mom began to recognize the symptoms of my eating disorder, she would subtly try to get me to eat by preparing my favorite dishes or by stocking the pantry with my favorite goodies. The smell of warm melted cheeses, hearty tomato sauce mixed with chunky mushrooms, and freshly baked garlic bread would often devour me as I would come home to find my mom cooking my favorite plate, three-cheese lasagna. My strength to abstain from food was certainly tempted. It took an immense amount of willpower on my part to stay as distant as I possibly could from my mom's lasagna. I would try to keep myself busy by cleaning, reorganizing, and categorizing every item in my room. The clothes in my closet were all color-coordinated, my shoes were neatly paired up. I would even add new hues to the items in my room in order to bring out the purple color of my walls. The time and energy that I spent in decorating my room kept me away from the delectable home-cooked meals that my mom prepared in our bright, sunny kitchen.

In order to keep myself from falling into these forbidden foods, I would first think of the feelings of guilt and self-hatred that I was likely to encounter if I chose to nourish my body in such a permissive manner.

"If you consume 100 more calories, consider yourself a failure . . . You want to get fat? Go ahead and eat that then . . . How could you have eaten all that, you fat cow? Look at yourself, there is fat plastered all over your body, it is pushing you outwards, slowly extending your soft skin another few inches . . .

Your bones are not as visible as they were yesterday!" These were all comments that Ana would reproach me with as I stood in front of the mirror that hung on the walls of my immaculate room. She would not allow me to eat a "normal" meal until I was able to see my hip bones, rib cage, and collarbones protruding from under my skin. I remember how I would rejoice with such pleasure as my bones became more visible because to me bones were a sign of beauty, a closer step to perfection.

The means that I learned to follow in order to rid my body of all visible fat were very extreme. They consisted of fasting, exercising until I felt faint, abusing laxatives, and a couple of times I also forced myself to purge. I feel secure in confessing, however, that it was only a couple of times that I actually purged my food. Purging often meant a lack of self-control, and my motto—"I don't care if it hurts, I want to have CONTROL, I want a perfect body, I want a perfect soul"—totally contradicted the act of purging. The times that I did vomit, however, I did it with all the defiance that I felt after bingeing. I wanted to rid my selfish body of everything it had consumed. I would kneel down on my knees, visualize the beautiful models that had become my thinspiration, stick my finger down my throat, and, after many attempts, see all the poison that I had put in my body come right back out and wash away down the sides of the toilet. In fact, the couple of times that I played this game only brought feelings of shame and embarrassment instead of the triumphant words that Ana would commend me with when I did not eat.

These punishments that I assigned myself after a binge were slowly giving rise to my beautiful suicide. It was a beautiful suicide because, although Ana was making me thinner and prettier, my health was also being severely threatened. However, I could not even imagine how I was ever going to eat again without feeling ashamed for betraying Ana. There came a time when I was aware of the damage that I was causing my body, but it was so difficult for me to leave Ana since both my body image and my mind were terribly distorted. This, I believe, has been the most difficult task to master.

It was going to take a lot of therapy to rid my mind of these feelings of guilt. In fact, it is something that up to this day still haunts me. Only I do not allow my punishments to be as destructive as they once were. After countless visits to my therapist, I learned that what nourishes my body, food, is not going to destroy me. I was forced to train my mind that it is not healthy to punish myself after a binge. Although it started off with a simple plan to lose five pounds, the power that I felt when I was in control took hold of me. My affinity to become thin, thinner, thinnest kept on growing each time I lost one more pound. Ana, the person I had once considered my "best friend," became my enemy, my disease. My family members and friends hated her while I secretly loved her. It was Ana who helped me get through my excruciating hunger pains, who made me thinner and more beautiful, but it was also Ana who created a loss in bone density, who created slow heart palpitations, who created a faulty and complicated image of my own body. Fortunate are those who can fully recover from anorexia nervosa. Although my health is no longer in danger as it once was, in other words I am a "recovered anorexic," there have been times when I have had relapses. Those feelings of guilt and that distorted image of my body have come back to haunt me. However, I am now more capable of fighting against that state of weakness, against a vulnerability to anorexia nervosa. I am aware that Ana is not a person. It is anorexia nervosa, a disease that kills.

Inglés in Thirty Minutes
James Espinoza

THE EVENING MY MOTHER SAW THE COMMERCIAL, she was ironing my sister's Catholic school uniform while watching a *novela*. My mother seemed to always be on her feet when she was at home: washing *chones*, grinding *chile* for salsa, or running around after my older sister and me. Even when we ate dinner, my mother often found herself standing, balancing a plate on one hand and, with the other, flipping *tortillas de maíz* on the *comal*. I used to think my mother preferred afternoons on her feet, having spent all day with her back slouched over a sewing machine at a Los Angeles garment factory.

At eight years of age, I remember my mother as motion, as if her body was all too aware of her hectic schedule. Her thick, black hair could never be flat or stagnant; its waves bounced off her shoulders to the rhythm of arms mashing pinto beans in corn oil, the premature white strands in her bangs dissolving in the bounce of the blackness. Even her clothes I recall in motion: the fluorescent flowers stitched on the squared collars of her peasant-type blouses were like smeared finger paints.

About the only time my mother would sit down on a weekday was when a brown van slowed past our chain-link fence and pulled into our driveway next to our swing set. A Mexican man would haul bundles of jean pants and pockets into our living room, drop them next to my mother's Singer, and thank her for taking the work. The Singer crowded a wall in our living room between windows with maroon curtains matching our carpet and reddening the pale pink of our walls. The needle of the machine would plunge into denim like a woodpecker's beak, the motor's roar blending in with the Spanish news on channel 34. And the machine's rage would shake everything in the room, like our framed picture of the Last Supper and my father's record player that on weekend mornings blared La Sonora Dinamita and Michael Jackson's "Thriller."

From my mother's at-home seamstress work, she earned ten cents a pocket, extra cash to help pay for our Catholic schooling at St. Matthias Elementary, where my sister and I learned English from nuns. I don't remember learning English, though, as if the whole process transpired within thirty minutes, too quick to bookmark the page. Yet I know it couldn't have been that easy, that somewhere there is a story about being caught between Spanish and English, and I get closer to understanding that story when I think of the *Inglés* in Thirty Minutes commercial.

When the commercial came on, I had just finished my St. Matthias homework on the dining room table. I had plopped belly-down in the living room and spread my He-Man action figures across the carpet. My sister, on the other hand, was never one to be preoccupied with play when watching television. On this particular evening, she was in her flannel pajamas, octagon-lensed glasses, and classic TV pose—elbows on carpet, chin resting on hands, and butt in the air. And my father, having eaten a late dinner after his overtime shift, rested on our tan sofa still in his work clothes, the obsidian shine of his straight hair dulled by the garment dust from a cutting room. He joked with my mother about a guy from his factory who had nearly been caught by *la migra* after stuttering gibberish in English.

When the *novelas* were on, conversations would only ensue during commercial breaks, and they would end mid-sentence once the melodrama of rich Pedros and poor but gorgeous Marías returned to the screen. This time, however, my mother stopped talking during a commercial. I followed her gaze to the squared tube, tuning my ears to the Spanish-speaking, over-enthusiastic, nonbreathing, disc jockey voice hypnotizing my mother:

"Are you tired of not having the job you feel you deserve? Are you tired of not living up to your potential? Well, ladies and gentlemen, your problems can be solved in thirty minutes. That's right. It's *Inglés* in Thirty Minutes, the fastest and easiest way to learn English. With only thirty minutes a day, you'll be speaking English and fulfilling your dreams within a year. For only $79.95 you'll receive twelve videotapes, six audiocassettes, three workbooks, and a bilingual dictionary. And that's not all. If you call now, we'll include a state-of-the-art audiocassette player absolutely free. You heard right. Absolutely free! All this for only $79.95. So what are you waiting for? We accept MasterCard, Visa, and American Express."

This verbosity was accompanied by images of a struggling fellow, someone like my mother or father, who had dished out the $79.95 and was downtrodden no more. He spoke English as well as any *pocho*, or any *güero* for that matter. By the end of the commercial, he wore a pin-striped suit and sunglasses because his future was too bright. (And he helped his children with their homework!) Surely, without effort, he could sing "Jingle Bells," unlike my mother, who during our Christmas show at St. Matthias, Mexicanized the carol into "*Chingo* bells, *chingo* bells, *chingo* aw da' way!"

Perhaps the look in my mother's eyes as she watched that commercial was foretelling. Could it be my mother already knew that years later, when she could no longer hide behind the expertise of her seamstress hands, when she got a new job working at a department chain store, she would learn to dread English-only staff meetings and impatient managers? Did she know that when customers would approach her with long-winded questions, she would squint her eyes trying to read their lips, ask for them to slow their speech, and finally nod, hoping her gesture was a satisfying response?

Yes, all along my mother must have known the necessity of English, a force ever-present like the rumbles from her sewing machine in our living room. To be successful, to wear the pinstripes and sunglasses, mastering English was the key. And for only $79.95 and thirty minutes a day, the key was within her grasp.

"Entonces, ¿qué crees, viejo? ¿Compramos ese curso de inglés?" my mother asked the night she had seen the commercial.

"Pero ¿te vas a poner a estudiar?" my father questioned. *"Siempre dices que vas a hacer esto y lo otro pero al último . . ."*

It didn't take much more to convince my father about the purchase of *Inglés* in Thirty Minutes. Three to four weeks later, the package arrived, Federal Express. When my mother got home from work, she took the box and set it on the edge of the dinner table along with the rest of the mail. No brown van pulled into our driveway, which meant the evening was open to begin her lessons. Of course, she went about her regular chores first. My mother couldn't stand a messy house or not providing a warm meal for us. This was evident every morning; she would wake up early to cook our breakfast *gorditas* smothered in sour cream. *"Tienen que comer para aprender,"* she would say.

But the evening the *Inglés* in Thirty Minutes package arrived, she went about her chores at an unprecedented speed, taking shortcuts as she deemed necessary. She cooked *chuletas de puerco* for all of us and ordered my sister to wash the dishes. She boiled the *frijoles* for the following morning with a higher flame. She mopped the floor, but didn't dry it. Still, by the time my mother finished her chores, the moon had chased the sun clear out of the sky.

My mother walked over to the table and picked up the package. She struggled to pull the flap off the box and grabbed a knife to stab at the stubborn tape. She opened the box and reached inside, causing a Styrofoam blizzard; white chunks flew as my mother pulled out our brand-new audiocassette player. I rushed toward the snowstorm as my sister entered through the hallway. We both lunged to grab the boom box while my mother held it aloft, curiously observing the spaceship-looking thing.

"Wow, Amá! Let me see it, 'Amá! *Hay que enchufarla pa' ver si trabaja,"* I exclaimed.

"Sí, Amá. Let me see it!" my sister repeated.

The two of us crowded over my mother and tugged at the defenseless audiocassette player. As we pulled on it, my father, who had been tending to the monthly bills in his bedroom but who simultaneously seemed to be everywhere, like God, wisely warned us to be careful. His voice, a mysterious force hidden in his slim body, boomeranged off the walls of our short hallway. But it was too late. The fast-forward button fell victim.

"¡Ya vieron! Miren, ya la quebraron," my mother scolded as she crouched down to search for the button amid the Styrofoam rubble. *"Ahora se me alistan para ir a la cama. Y Jimmi, recoge todos esos jugetes que están tirados en el piso."*

"But Amá, *todavía ni son las* nine-thirty," my sister and I uselessly argued.

"¡Acostarse!" my father ordered.

My mother returned her attention to the box. She pulled out the video and audiocassette tapes one by one, the covers decorated in patriotic red stripes and blue letters, and each piece numbered for a smooth transition between Spanish and English. Then she thumbed through the three workbooks and the dictionary. After sharpening a couple of pencils, she walked to our junk closet and snatched a yellow notebook.

I had seen such notebooks many times. I would run into them whenever I misplaced a watch or a He-Man plastic sword and rummaged through our closet. Each notebook recorded yet another failed attempt at English literacy. The purple one was from her days at a night school in East Los Angeles when she had recently arrived in the United States. Her only form of transportation back then was the bus. The adult school classes ended late, and she worried about taking the bus alone, especially after a close call with three drunks. The blue one was used in conjunction with a grammar workbook she bought or borrowed from a friend. The book was so advanced it frustrated her, so she stashed it in the closet.

And the red one marked her independent study phase. My mother would write down verbs in their present, past, and future tense over and over again. She seemed to believe that if she endlessly listed the various forms of "to be," they would be tattooed in her memory and emerge when a conversation warranted the verb's proper use. She also practiced writing her numbers in expanded form so she wouldn't have to refer to her little cheat sheet or ask my sister and me to write checks for her at the grocery store.

But now there was the yellow notebook. The yellow one signaled a new era, the promise of *Inglés* in Thirty Minutes.

She slid the tape labeled "Number 1" into the VCR. She turned on the televison and pushed every button on both the televison and VCR except for the right one. "Jimmy," my mother called out, *"¿Cómo se prende esta cosa?"*

I set the televison to channel 3 and pressed play. A peppered screen appeared, and after a second or so, a tacky jingle filled the room. The melody was synchronized with an exaggerated display of computer graphics dancing on the screen and spelling out *"Inglés* in Thirty Minutes."

"Ahhh, okey, gracias," my mother said, *"Ahora vete a lavar los dientes para que te vayas a acostar."*

I made my way into the bathroom, and as I turned to go inside, I saw something I don't recall happening too often: my mother sat down.

From the bathroom, I heard a stern voice announce, "Lesson number one, greetings. Please repeat . . . How are you?"

"How are jew?" my mother repeated.

"Fine. How about you?"

"Fine. How abow jew?"

"Amá," I called out to her, *"¡no puedo encontrar mi cepillo!"*

"I'm doing great, thank you."

"Está en . . . I doin' gray, thank jew . . . *¡el cajón de en medio!"*

After brushing my teeth, I peeked into the living room and chuckled. On the screen appeared an instructor who wore cream khakis and a buttoned-up green shirt a size too small. He waved a skinny white wand in front of a blackboard strategically placed there to enhance the educational vibe, but the classroom could have easily been an attic or a mechanic's garage.

The comedy didn't end there. Sometimes when my parents weren't watching, my sister and I played certain parts of the videotapes for a cheap laugh. The English course claimed to provide simulated, real-life situations when the English terms and phrases introduced by the instructor came in handy. What made these skits entertaining was the horrendous acting and the dialogue cheesier than nachos. These skits made our nightly *novelas* seem like theater masterpieces. I remember we played one scene repeatedly. A woman and a man (perhaps the same instructor guy, but now wearing glasses and a hat) walked around a house looking for common objects.

"Where is my shoe?" inquired the man.

"It is under the bed," said the woman dressed in classic 80s attire and flaunting wild blonde locks.

"Where are my keys?" asked the man after putting on his missing shoe.

"They are on the table," replied the big-haired woman.

"Where is my spoon?" the forgetful man asked.

"It is in the kitchen drawer."

My sister and I would then walk around the house wearing only one shoe and asking random questions:

"Where is my hat?" I asked.

"It is on your head, *nerdo*," my sister responded.

"Where is my house?"

"It is on the street, *nerdo*."

"Why do I lose everything?"

"Cuz' you're a *nerdo, nerdo*." My sister had recently developed a nickname for me—*nerdo*. It was her Spanglish term for nerd. It made sense, I suppose, given that every word she was prohibited to use to refer to me ended in the letter o, from *tonto* to *menso* to *pendejo*.

My mother continued her lessons on and off depending on her at-home workload for about a month. She dealt with our interruptions and my father occasionally asking her to come to bed. Then, one night, as sleep crept into me, I remember hearing my mother reciting the alphabet in English upon cue from the video instructor:

"L . . . M . . . N . . . O . . . P"

Suddenly, her voice vanished. I lay there for a moment waiting for accented letters to rise from the silence of the night, but all I heard was the instructor. I roused from bed to investigate. My mother sat on the couch, her notebook and dictionary sprawled on the coffee table like opened butterfly wings, her eyes peacefully shut, her hair as calm as a puddle on a windless day. I stared at my mother's stillness.

Did she dream about English spilling from her tongue like a river flowing? Or were her dreams also drowned in the rattles of a sewing machine, the bubbling water of *frijoles* in a pot, the screams of my sister and me chasing an ice-cream truck?

A part of me wanted to wake my mother up, let her know it hadn't been thirty minutes. But the other part of me walked over to the televison and turned it off. The next night she fell asleep within fifteen minutes; then it was ten, then five, and then all twelve videotapes found their way back to their box and into our closet. The only thing remaining was the audiocassette player with its missing fast-forward button.

un pedazo de mi vida se fue
nick gaitan

I GRABBED MY GRANDMOTHER'S SHAKING HAND. I didn't have the courage to look her in the eye. It was one of those things that the family had thought we were prepared for. I flashed back to the last birthday my grandfather had before becoming bedridden. There were also images in my mind of the stomping bar fighter, the boxer. I also remembered sitting on his lap as a boy, looking at his tough knuckles, listening to him and my own father talking. Now, I was standing over his motionless body in the hospital bed, and there was only silence. It was a hush that could never be reproduced. My grandfather was dead, as dead as the leaves of fall in the bone yard where concrete angels weep. His face was empty, and I was concerned with insignificant things like my tears landing on his white hospital sheet. His mouth would get my attention at one point because of the way it was stiffly and crookedly open. I can't even tell why I would be so preoccupied with these specific details. I suppose these things happen, but now I can't make any sense of it.

The night before, I had hung up the phone after finishing up all of the day's simpler things. Just gathering a few friends, three or four, that's all. We would hang out, get something to drink, and have a good time. You know the nights, the ones when you close your parents' bedroom door just in case one of the friends you bring over wanders. You put away those expensive bottles that Dad hasn't opened yet, and you make goddamned sure that there ain't no shit gonna get lost or lifted. Moonlight and madness took us for a ride into the night that must have ended at some point none of us remember. When I was turning light switches off, I would find one after the other passed out on a couch or the floor. I had wondered if they would be disappearing throughout the night. I could only smile, thinking these lousy bastards must have dropped after taking the late night piss that every drunk takes before falling into a mumbling slumber.

That phone had a ring like a choking turkey in a bad dream. I realized I had fallen asleep on the couch in the living room. It was Uncle George. "Hey Nicky, Grandpa got sick and we're following the ambulance to the hospital." My heart sank. I tried to get in touch with my brother and sister and managed to find only one of them. My sister would leave her home and start on her way over to where I was. All I could do was wait. That was the worst feeling I have ever felt, knowing that the world was not right and having to wait on others before I could even do anything about it. The sounds of the living room ceiling fan and a Brook Benton record on the stereo were the only things filling the air.

I ran out into the backyard. I started cleaning up the aluminum cans, then I went to the bottles. The buzzing flies, the smell of dog shit and beer in the hot morning sun were the only things pounding my hung-over senses. I would feel nausea every now and then because of the horrible smells while I was back there trying to clean up. When I came in for water, I noticed that I missed a call. The message left on my parents' machine sent my mind a thousand miles at speeds I have never known. It was Uncle George again. "Nick, you have to get in touch with your dad. Grandpa is gone . . . " There was a quick silence followed by words I couldn't make out and the click. I truly believe the entire universe must have stopped momentarily. I went around the house waking all of my friends, saying something went wrong. I watched them stagger out the front door one by one with no questions. I called my sister Gina back in a hurry. She had found my brother by the time I called her back, and they were on their way over to the house. In a frantic sadness I cannot describe to this day, I went out back again. I started cleaning cigarette butts and roaches between the bricks and on the table. What in the world was I thinking? Who cared about all these things at a time like this? I didn't give it a thought at that time.

My brother walked in with my niece and I didn't know what he would say. I never know what he is going to say when someone has died. We hugged tightly, and then I felt his tense body start to swing at the arms. His fists hit the walls, scaring my niece who was behind him. Over his shoulder I could see her little bottom lip curl in fear and sadness. I whispered to him that she was frightened and he managed to cool down. Terrified, we wanted to hear the phone ring, but then again we didn't. See, Mom and Dad were in Florida, and this was the worst part about the entire thing.

We had called them earlier but didn't get an answer. With a stroke of luck, although I don't think it is the right choice of words to describe what happened, the phone rang. It was my father that I heard on the other end. I couldn't even get a word out before I was handing the phone to my brother. I swear to God that this phone conversation was the longest I have ever heard anyone take part in, but it must have been less than ten minutes. I could hear the screaming voice of my father straight through the air. I hung my head as tears started to fall. That sound pierced straight through my soul and I couldn't do a thing about it.

Within thirty minutes we drove, parked, and walked into those doors at Ben Taub. I hated saying these words; I hated hearing them. All it meant when someone said "Ben Taub" was that there was going to be bad news. When we got off the elevator, we found the room and I could hear my grandmother weeping before we opened the door. I broke down once again. The grey shades that were about the room saturated us in sadness. In the midst of all the sounds and tears, I saw that my grandfather's jaw was not shut. This bugged me badly and I leaned over him, pushing it shut. I look back now and don't know the reason for such a concern. I suppose I didn't want the world to see him this way. It might have been my pride pushing his face shut so he wouldn't look dead. The truth would remain that he was, obviously, and I think that this was really my problem. The power of denial could not save me.

In the eternity of Saturday morning, I started to realize it would be complete hell on my father. I was thinking of every last story that he had told me about his own father. I kept flashing to my times as a kid and Dad showing me photos of Clayton Homes in the 50s—the *pachucos* with pompadours dark and high with grease and Schwinn bikes in the background. I started to remember the way my grandfather would smile all day when people were around.

Time was at a complete standstill, everything around me seemed to be as sad as I was. The stereo still had the Brook Benton record on it. It played and played. I heard "A Rainy Night in Georgia." Shit, between that sad song and everything else that was happening, there was a goddamned storm on all of life itself. I started to imagine the faces my grandfather would make to trip us out as kids. He would do this thing where he turned his nose up and pulled his cheeks down, making his eyes sag something horrible.

I just started laughing out loud and my sister looked up in disbelief. "What . . . ?" And then she started laughing herself. What a strange moment—it left as easy as it came. We must have both been thinking of some of those funny things he would do to make us laugh. Grandpa was some character, and it's just a funny thing how memories of him are always dressed in the sharpest *guayaberas* and Stacy Adams shoes, black and shiny, reflecting the sidewalks of the world that he walked upon.

Time had passed for only a few distinct seconds before I started to cry again, wondering how my father was going to see the situation. I really didn't know what to think and that was what scared the hell out of me.

The funeral service was surreal to me. I saw my grandfather in the coffin. During his last days he was in his hospital bed, an amputee, bearded and lost in his mental condition. He had been deteriorating slowly, and the stubble turned to a full white beard. When I looked at him now, in a suit, shaven, with high cheekbones, it was different. The picture they had placed in his open coffin was taken during the 1940s in his Army uniform. This was what he looked like before I was born. It was beautiful and frightening at the same time how this man's face had remained physically young.

Later, after the service, the black coach would lead the motorcade down the winding road of the graveyard. It was a silent day, clear outside. Lots of faces that we hadn't seen since years ago. I remember the service outside, made brief for the fear that my grandmother would collapse. She never did well at funerals, much less at the funeral of the love of her life. My father had it the worst in my eyes. His only wish had been to be with his father during his last hours. This was all he wanted and hoped for. But, in came death while he was gone, leaving reminders of sweet, sweet life. I was once a child in grandfather's arms; I ended up as his pallbearer. We drove home shortly after he was put into the ground.

swimming lessons
cristina A. gomez

I REMEMBER THE SUMMERS when my mother used to enroll us in swimming lessons at the municipal pool. It was always at least a million degrees outside, and we dreaded the barefoot run from the car to the pool. The concrete made us dance like an old western villain was shooting at our feet. None of it mattered when we got to the water though. It was soothing, and you could practically see the steam rise once you dipped your feet in the water. My sister and brother would have to sit on the edge and dangle their feet until their coach got there, but I had much more swimming experience and was able to swim wherever I pleased.

I was in the deep end this particular day. Victor and Crystal, about six and seven years old, were floating around in the shallow end at the opposite end of the pool. I remember climbing the ladder and thinking about my next dive. I walked out on the end of the board and bounced to get a feel for the spring. I stepped back a couple of steps to aid the force of my hop. I stepped forward, hopped, and then I heard it. I heard the screaming. The familiar pitch of the scream distracted me and took my eyes from the sky. I looked over to the shallow end and felt my feet hit the board. I sprung off. I was launched in no particular direction with no particular technique or grace. I was trying to see what was going on at the shallow end of the pool. Recognizing a cry for help must be something embedded in a family's genetic code. You always know their voices, you can predict what they are going to say, and you can recognize their screams. It isn't that they even have to say anything; for me it was hearing my sister and brother choking on chlorinated water. I had never heard them choke before, but the instant I heard their gurgles, I knew. When I was underwater, I knew I had to get back up. I had to find out what was going on. I couldn't get up fast enough—I was kicking and kicking—it's then I realized how deep the water was. When I resurfaced, I heard the screaming again. I heard my name being yelled. I swam to the edge of the pool, pulled myself out, and ran to the other end. The rule—no running around the pool—didn't apply to me. My family was in danger. I looked over and saw that both my brother and sister were frantically splashing around trying to keep their heads above water.

My brother and sister, who don't openly show affection, were crying to each other. "It's okay, Victor! I'm right here!"

"I love you—just hold on!"

"I'm here for you!"

They were so afraid they were going to drown—even if it was virtually impossible with overinflated floaties and the number of lifeguards working with the younger children.

"You're okay!" I yelled to them. "Just calm down. You have floaties on!" And then their faces changed. They were scared but I was there now. Their big sister was there, and they knew even though we argued and I picked on them, I wouldn't let anything happen to them. "Victor, you need to calm down—it's only four feet deep!" They tried to find me at the edge of the pool but the life jackets prevented peripheral vision, and the floaties on their arms didn't allow them the liberty to swim freestyle to the ledge. They had only been about five inches from the ledge when they started to panic. I reached over and grabbed their arms, pulling them toward the ledge. "Here, hold on to this," I said, placing their little hands on the concrete. I lifted Victor out of the pool and sat him down. I turned to Crystal. She was a little heavier— our little *gordis*. I looked up at a lifeguard right behind me; and he helped me lift her. I took them from the pool, sat them down on the bleachers, and took their life jackets and arm floaties off. They were coughing up water, and their poor little eyes were red from the chlorine. They hugged me, and while most of the time I didn't like my brother and sister to hug me, I didn't mind so much this time.

◆

Years later, I would make my brother feel really bad about himself, as older overbearing sisters have a tendency to do. "You are so lazy!" I would yell at him. He would sit on the couch and just stare at the television, ignoring me, making me scream even louder, "This is why you don't do well in school. You're stupid and lazy!"

And in a fight with my sister over the remote, I would break her front tooth on our new tile floor. The tile that originally shimmered mother-of-pearl would become slippery with her blood.

I remember her watching a television show and stepping out of the room to go to the kitchen. I walked in, sat in her seat, and changed the channel, knowing completely well that she had just been there and would be right back.

"Nany, I was sitting there."

"So?"

"So, move," she said, trying to take the remote away from me. I jerked it back and accidentally hit her in the head. Angry, she grabbed my arms and we ended up wrestling on the couch. I threw her off of me, and she landed face first on the new tile floor. Her front tooth was broken in half and instantaneously the blood started pouring out of her mouth.

We never tell the story about how I broke Crystal's tooth in half or how I systematically might have affected my brother's self-esteem. We tell the swimming lesson story. The story of how I saved their lives—even though their lives were never really in danger. Every time we tell the story, they smile. A smile that says to me, "We know you love us." And I do.

Life by *seventeen*

Jynelle A. Gracia

IN KINDERGARTEN I WANTED TO BE A LIFEGUARD so badly my mother had no choice but to let me go dressed as one to Career Day in Mrs. Dahne's class, even though we both knew I couldn't swim and going to school in a bathing suit was against the dress code. By second grade, I wanted to be a teacher like my mother. It was an occupation she hadn't picked. In an act of miraculous intervention, the priest had recognized her promise among the graduates in the parish, driven her to the university that was then Texas A&I, and told her where she would live, what she would study, and where to sign the loan forms. In a flash, college, and a wholly different life, was possible. Maybe because my parents wanted to encourage in me the choices they didn't feel they'd had, they tolerated my announcing a different profession each time one occurred to me: pediatrician, dancer, magician's assistant, nun. My parents have them all written down in a coil-bound scrapbook called School Days, where my weight and height, after-school activities, and the names of my friends are written underneath each wallet-sized school photo. Like all kind, hopeful parents who lie to their children, they would always say, year after year, *Yes, of course, you can be anything you want to be.*

In eighth grade, when my parents let me subscribe to *Seventeen* magazine, I told my father I wanted to be a model. He said that was fine, but that I'd have to be a plus-size model, like the ones wearing dark, shapeless pants with elastic waistbands, not in these glossy pages but in the garish K-Mart circulars that were the guts of the Sunday *Caller-Times*. He reminded me that I was 5'2" and wore a size 10. He took my magazine and compared my face with the woman on the cover. Her cheeks sloped in where mine were round like peaches. *But she's not smiling*, I argued, and sucked in the sides of my mouth. He pointed out how her thigh was the size of my forearm.

I didn't want to model ugly clothes, so—fickle as ever—I decided to aim instead for editor-in-chief. My English teacher had a bookshelf full of his family's old magazines at the back of his classroom. Each day, I would finish my work early so I could go to the bookshelf and scour *National Geographic, The New Yorker, Cosmopolitan*, and *Texas Monthly*. Mr. Brown noticed my habit, and I told him that one day it would be my name atop the *Seventeen* masthead. He said it was a wonderful career choice, but that I should consider other publications, something more serious. He nodded toward the bookcase.

Seventeen was serious enough. There were articles on subjects I didn't encounter in the semirural outskirts of Corpus Christi where I lived: a woman who lamented being labeled a "Jewish American Princess" (there was one kid, Colin Turner, who was Jewish but he'd moved away in fourth grade), women who had survived rape (that word simply wasn't uttered), interracial couples who had experienced hate crimes, girls who ran 5Ks in honor of mothers they'd lost to breast cancer. Of course, lives like these probably were being lived near me, but those realities felt miles away from my house that sat on a cul-de-sac. Most people who drove to the end of our street had made a mistake, so they circled around and headed back down the hill. Our high school loomed over cornfields that stretched for miles until your sight clanged against the colossal silver smokestacks of the refineries that interrupted the horizon. If you got on the highway and drove away from the refineries, you ended up at the beach. Those were the parameters of my world. A dead end. The corn fields. The Gulf.

I could escape for a while reading the fiction in *Seventeen*. I remember clearly a story about a "good girl" who became enchanted with a "bad girl," who had taken her under her wing in the high school social scene. The bad girl made her own perfumes out of vanilla, spices, and rubbing alcohol, and drove a green convertible. With the money she earned at her job at a pizza shop, she bought CDs and clothes she picked out herself, and on the days she got off work early, she didn't go straight home. She walked around the city she lived in and talked to strangers. No one I knew walked anywhere, unless it was exercise. Busy streets lined with businesses and pedestrians were exotic, mysterious, and limitless to me. The graphic on the opening page of the story showed the bad girl dark-haired, leather-jacketed, and confident, driving into the night in a green convertible. She was such a bad-ass, the wheels on her car didn't even touch the road. The good girl at her side looked worried, hands pressed against her orange bob to keep her hair in place, as they soared. She'd lied to her parents that night in order to go to a party with the bad girl's pizza shop friends, where she watched the bad girl prove her good side by not letting a guy who'd been drinking beer drive home. No question which character I wanted to be, and—wasn't this why I loved reading?— when I read that story, those were my shoulders snug in that leather jacket; it was my hair whipping around like a flag in a storm as I raced around my town.

I would study carefully the author bios printed at the end of the short stories: "Lisa Somebody is a senior at Columbia University in New York City." Or: "Linda Somebodyelse is a freelance writer and frequent contributor to *Seventeen*." Sometimes, and this is what excited me most, the stories were winners of contests the magazine held.

I thought I was a pretty good writer, but not good enough to win. I had several trophies from Ready Writing competitions held after school in the library of our junior high, but it was easy to win those. The topics were broad. I included literary references from whatever I happened to be reading in Mr. Brown's class at the time, threw in some similes and metaphors, and that was pretty much it. We only had two hours to write the essays, so the judges only had two hours' worth of expectations. But I knew I was too inexperienced to write meaningful stories for people who actually dated and had jobs. I wouldn't realize until I was actually seventeen that women eighteen and older who were interested in these kinds of magazines read sophisticated *Vogue* and *Harper's Bazaar* or racier *YM*—where the headlines weren't concerned with Dating, but with Orgasms. But at that time, I thought I'd be found out as a phony if I tried to write what I could only imagine, especially if I had to write thousands of words about it. I resigned myself to wait until I'd entered those worlds and lived that vocabulary. Besides, I'd never written anything thousands of words long.

A contest in that year's September issue gave me my big break. That month's issue was always thicker (like the Prom issue in April), the budding editor in me noticed, because it was packed with back-to-school fashion trends and (aha!) thousands of ads. I don't remember what the contest's prize was. That wasn't important. *Seventeen*, along with a corporate sponsor, Noxzema probably, was holding an essay competition to honor a young woman for her outstanding community service. Entrants were to describe their service in an essay one hundred words or less, and the magazine would feature an article, with photographs, about the winner.

I could write one hundred words easy, I thought. I wrote my essay about working at the local AIDS hospice and my commitment to AIDS awareness. Sitting on my bed in my bedroom, I wrote in longhand on yellow legal paper, using the magazine opened to the contest guidelines as my writing surface. In carefully chosen words, I described a patient with whom I'd grown close before she passed away. I described the courage she'd had and the symbiotic relationship we'd forged. I remember using the adjective "symbiotic," figuring it was a marathon runner of a word, and using a thesaurus to muscle up the rest of the prose. I wrote sentences as they came naturally, then went back and crossed out half the words. All of my hopes to appear in my favorite magazine—to embark on my career in magazines, I thought—were packed into a paragraph fifty-seven words shorter than this one.

We had an Apple IIc in the dining room we hardly ever used, but I didn't dare type the essay. The printer whined across every line so loudly you could hear it even in the bathroom with the door closed and the shower running, and I didn't want anyone to know what I was working on. I folded my neatest copy, addressed and stamped the envelope, and then laid back in my bed, daydreaming about which outfit I would wear in the photograph they would run in the announcement. I dreamed that the editors would request more of my work or offer me a summer job. Or maybe they would decide I could be a model, after all.

The thing was, I had never set foot inside any AIDS hospice. I had read (in *Seventeen*, of course. I remember the article clearly) profiles of young women who had contracted HIV, and it was the most terrifying thing you could tell a girl who was secretly starting to think about having sex. I'd learned that there was an AIDS hospice in our city and decided to volunteer. When I'd told my mother of my plans, there was none of the usual support. Instead, she flipped out into Spanish—*¿Estás loca, o qué?*—even though she'd just been talking quietly in English with my brother. My father, outwardly much calmer than my mother, told me that my schoolwork was the only work I needed to worry about. Besides being an editor-in-chief, I'd argued, I also really wanted to be a doctor, so I needed to get started on internships (another word I'd learned from the magazine) and volunteering. Those were the things I had to do in order to make it into a premed program when I applied to college. Didn't he understand?

I'd gone to my file boxes, where I'd organized my issues, and tried to find the one containing the AIDS article. I couldn't find it, so I informed my parents on the statistics I remembered. My mother set her clenched fists on her hips as I reminded her of the ways HIV was and wasn't contracted, and she did that silly thing she always did with my words when she wanted to put me in my place: I got your "risky behavior" right here, young lady. I think my parents might have been pleasantly terrified that I was educating them, the same way they are bewildered today at the questionably legal things my brother can do with computers. Despite my pleading, they countered with one argument I couldn't dispute. I didn't drive yet, the hospice was twenty-five minutes away, each way, and one of them would have to haul me there and pick me up. It was as unrealistic as asking for a flying green convertible. End of discussion (or so they thought).

The post office was seven blocks away from my house, and I planned to mail my essay after school the day after I'd finished it. It was all I could think about for the next twenty hours. Receiving congratulations on *Seventeen* letterhead, seeing my essay in print, ordering extra copies for my friends, how busted I was going to be. The magazine staff would find me out for the fraud I was once they called for an interview and spoke with my parents. When the fact-checker called the volunteer director of the clinic—as I had, to determine her name so I could write it on the entry form—she would have no idea who I was. I decided not to send it.

But what if I did send it and I didn't win? My imagined life in one hundred words would not be fact-checked, but only read by someone, maybe an editorial assistant or a Noxzema PR intern, and then it would sit in a file with the other rejects, not good enough, my imagined life not exactly what they were looking for, but *fully believed*. Not impressive, but unquestionably banal. It didn't matter if it was only one other person who read it and believed it. It didn't matter that that version of me could live only in the seemingly insignificant realm of the contest-world. Not winning the contest was my only chance at having, in some tiny way, the life I wanted. I had to send it.

When I got home from school the next day, I fed my dog and took a shower. I changed my clothes, ate the *migas* my mom made, and, to my brother's surprise, agreed to watch him beat Bowser at the end of Super Mario Bros. again. Then I went to my room, started on my homework, and talked on the phone. I let it get late. I let days go by, weeks. When the deadline passed, I told myself I'd done the right thing not entering the contest, because in my refinery-and-cornfield-bound mind I was convinced I would have won, and when I did win, my imagined life would be scandalized. I left that letter on my desk so long the address started to bleed and the envelope yellowed. Even though it sat in clear sight, I eventually stopped seeing it.

If I had thought more about it, I would have thrown the entry away because, like all well-meaning, over-interested parents, my mother couldn't see a letter addressed to *Seventeen* magazine sit on my desk indefinitely. One evening, long after I'd forgotten about it, I walked into my room and found her standing by my desk with the opened envelope in one hand. Oh shit, I'm in deep shit, I thought, suddenly deeply embarrassed by my precociousness. I'll just tell her it's fiction. I could see that she was laughing a little, but also that some kind of tears were draining her mascara into the creases around her mouth and she was holding onto the back of my chair. Those tears relieved me. Whether she was crying from laughing too hard or from pitying me, I was safe either way. In her easiest voice she promised that I could volunteer somewhere next summer, if I wanted. She would drive me wherever I needed to go, no problem, since it was summer break and she wouldn't be working, and no, it wouldn't be any problem at all, even if my father didn't like the idea, not to worry, just as long as it wasn't too far away.

The car story
valarie Hurtado

TÍA MARY LOU WAS GORGEOUS. When I think about her, I remember the way she looked—the way I wished she still looked. Her sun-kissed skin was a golden olive tone. Her eyes a chocolate brown, warming every room she entered. Her hair, a dark brown with bits and pieces of grey here and there, was filtered with the scents of gardenias. Not only was she striking to the eye, but once you met Tía, you would never forget her. There was not a time where her beauty, combined with her hard-headedness, couldn't either get her out of a jam or persuade anyone to see things her way. Tía was born in Mexico, and later moved to the East Side of Houston. Growing up, she was surrounded by a large Hispanic community that was close-knit and inviting. There were small corner stores that she and her siblings would visit often in the neighborhood with Abuelita, so everyone knew them and their parents. Everyone knew that Tía was determined and strong-minded because they watched her grow up. She managed to leave her impression everywhere she went, like the way she left her impression on the insurance agent and the car salesman.

It all started when she decided she wanted to learn how to drive. By way of her mentality, the first thing she had to do is get insurance, then she could purchase a car, and then she could learn how to drive. Who on earth tries to get insurance before they purchase a car? All of her brothers and sisters were well aware that she could not take no for an answer. So when they tell this story, they tell of how they knew she would be coming home with insurance and a brand-new car.

Instead of her riding the bus, Tío Victor decided to drive her on this wild escapade. Tío had been given the duty of taking care of his sisters and helping them whenever they needed him. And this time was no exception, he was the chosen brother. I believe that he and Tía Mary Lou shared the same charismatic personalities. However, this time around even he was surprised. Of course, the entire time, *él pensaba que ella estaba loca, pero*, she knew what she was doing and he knew that she would do it. I can almost hear it as if I were there, her voice saying, "Well, sir, I must have insurance to buy a car and I need a car to learn how to drive." Tío said that he just stood back and watched her reason with the guy.

I can only imagine the way she worked her magic on him. I can see her sitting straight up in her chair in front of the insurance agent, with her hands strategically placed on her lap to display her soft hands and manicured nails. I can't remember a time when I looked at her hands and they didn't look beautiful. It made me want mine to look just like hers. It's almost as if I can see her there with this serious look on her face while she pleaded with the agent. Tía's look was so unique it's almost indescribable. She would gaze at you with these piercing brown eyes that forced you to keep your attention on her. It was almost as if you would lose your train of thought, forget what she was saying, and just agree with her. I'm certain that the insurance agent found himself in her trance, which is why she left his office with the car insurance. By the end of the day, Tío says, she had a brand-new car and insurance to go along with it. I wish I could have been there to see her work her magic; I would have taken notes.

I mentioned before how I remember the way I wish she could have always looked. Well, it's because the breast cancer changed her. Instead of her beautiful, healthy, sun-kissed glow, she became pale and sallow. I guess the radiation and chemotherapy exhausted her completely.

So why did this have to happen to her? Who can answer that for me? To me, she was like all the other women in my family, invincible. I remember the way she fought and lived with cancer for so many years. That is why when I heard her car story, it did not surprise me one bit. Even though she was battling breast cancer, she still managed to receive Teacher of the Year in Bilingual Education from the Houston Independent School district —the largest one in Houston. I mean, come on, who can do something like that? This just proves to me that her strength to fight was incredible and she never gave up in the face of adversity. Her strength kept her alive, all the way to the end of her exhausted battle. We all knew that she was extremely sick, I just had not thought about the fact that she could, one day, die. We are all going to die sometime; it just catches you by surprise when it happens to someone you love. I watched her get better and go through a five-year remission. I just knew that the cancer was gone; she was going to be fine. But when we least expected it, the breast cancer spread like wildfire through her renewed strong body. It took her over this time, and she did not have the last word. The cancer did.

At her memorial service, all I can remember are the vivid images I have of every single person coming up to the podium, one after the other. Her fellow colleagues spoke of how her beautiful spirit had an effect on them. In particular, I remember a thin, beautiful Hispanic woman who spoke in Spanish about how Tía's legacy keeps her going. She was one of Tía's students who, through the assistance and encouragement of Tía, went to medical school and became a doctor.

Do you know how when someone you love is just gone, obviously you know that they are not there anymore, and you cannot fathom what the hell's going on? Well, I went through that for a while. I'm okay now. I want to say that I know she is at a place that is better than anyone could ever possibly imagine.

I have a picture of her in my room, right by my door next to the light switch. It is there so that I can be reminded of her each day I leave my room. Thinking back to her—especially the car story—I remember that I want to be strong like her, fight my battles the way she fought hers, and even leave this earth with a legacy.

see you when god says so

YOU KNOW HOW THERE IS ALWAYS something that your grandparents say or do, like a funny joke that you can never forget? My Grandpa would always ask me, "Hey, *m'ija*, how old are you?" Then, of course, I would tell him my age, and he would reply, "Me, I'm twenty-five," and it would always make me laugh. Thinking back I can remember standing there in the living room of his small apartment, staring up at this giant towering over me holding up two fingers on one hand and five on the other. For a while when I was younger, I didn't know any better and I believed him.

We spent every Thanksgiving and Christmas together as a family. Uncle Marcus, my dad's brother, would always cook lavish meals that you could smell as soon as you walked into his house. My favorite scent was Uncle's green mint fruit salad. Just like a kid, that was the first thing that I went to see, the dessert table, and there it was, my favorite salad. I would get close to it, sniff the mint aroma, and then anticipate its flavor hitting my taste buds. This was one of my favorite times to be with Grandpa. He was a strong man who always made me feel protected and who always made me laugh. Even though he was older, Grandpa was on the go, moving around and joking with us. This is why he was strong to me; he wasn't like other Grandpas, who seemed old and frail.

To him, I was his *princesa*, and my sister, Veronica, was his *reina*. I remember this the most during Christmastime, because it was then that Grandpa called for us by these names. When I think back, it's like I can almost hear his voice, filled with a bit of raspyness, yet still tender enough to make my sister and I come running for our presents. After we ate dinner, we all sat around the living room opening presents and listening to Christmas music. Grandpa's favorite song was "The Drummer Boy." We all knew that this song was a given at Christmastime, so when it came on I always focused my attention on him. He sat up straight and tall in the dark brown leather La-Z-Boy with me on his lap. His arms and hands were extended and resting on the chair's arms. He didn't move much during the song. He just sat there in silent tranquility enjoying every beat of the drum. I remember sitting there and looking at his hands. They had dark brown spots on them. As a kid I really didn't know what these were—now I know they were age spots—but back then I thought that my Grandpa was special because of his brown spots. I liked looking at them because even though the spots were there, his hands were still soft and gentle. I never wanted the song to end; I wanted to sit there forever on his lap because I felt so secure and loved.

I don't quite remember the last Christmas that we spent together. However, there are things that I do remember about the last few years of his life that won't ever go away.

My father and uncles decided that Grandpa needed to live in a nursing home. This way he could have special care and activities with other senior citizens. I was only about seven or eight years old. I have this memory that always comes to mind when I think about his time in the nursing home. He used to call us every day just to say hello. There was something additional that he did that I just absolutely loved—he used to call to ask what time it was. This is how each of the phone calls would go: "Hello," "Hi, *m'ija* it's me. What time is it?" "It's three o' clock." "Okay, *m'ija*, thank you. Bye-bye." I can imagine the smile that was on his face as he talked to us. I'm sure that it extended from ear to ear with his eyebrows raised, like when he lied about his age. Now when I think back on those moments, I feel as if they are some of my fondest memories as well as the saddest reminders of Grandpa. It was just a simple phone call, but I looked forward to it every day.

The phone calls became fewer and fewer until finally I don't remember receiving them anymore. I wanted to go to visit him, but my dad would always go very early in the morning without any of us. I used to get so angry with him and wondered why he never took me to see Grandpa. At night I would loll in bed and pray to God that Grandpa wasn't mad at me because I never went to see him. I would think about the way he looked, the way his room might have looked at the nursing home, what he wore, and I'd wonder if he had any friends. I didn't want him to think that I'd forgotten him or that I didn't love him anymore. I was a kid. How was I supposed to know any better? Finally, one day my oldest sister, Vanessa, went with my dad to visit Grandpa. She really didn't talk too much about the visit when she came home. Later on I found out why. He didn't remember who she was; he had to keep asking my dad questions. I know now that my dad was just trying to protect my memory of Grandpa. He didn't want us to see him that way. I don't think I would have wanted us to either.

It was probably about a year after that visit that we got a phone call early in the morning. I remember answering the phone and it being Uncle Marcus. He asked to speak with my dad. I didn't expect it to be THE phone call, but it was. On that September day, the time had come for Grandpa's journey to end. The weird thing about it is I don't remember how I was told about his passing. All I remember that morning after the phone call is going to the kitchen and getting some *pan dulce,* taking it to my room, and slowly eating it as the tears rolled down my face onto my plate. I sat there as the tears collected into a small puddle on the plate, soaking the *pan dulce* that I continued to stuff mindlessly into my mouth. Then I waited my turn to take a shower so that we could go to the hospital. The next recollection I have is the tortuous car ride to the hospital. I wanted to get there but I really didn't want to get there. Finally, we arrived at the hospital. Of course, we waited in the small waiting room with grey walls, small sofas, and small TVs to watch—for what seemed like an eternity. I remember everything looked so miniscule to me. I guess for the first time in my life I wasn't interested in the scenery. It was gloomy to me anyway. One by one, we were allowed to go in and see him before they took him to the funeral home. At first I was scared, and I wasn't sure if it was a good idea to go and see him, but boy, am I glad I did.

I remember his long body lying there so peacefully and serene with his eyes closed, almost looking as if he were just sleeping. How I wished that were the case. I stared at him for a good five minutes; I wanted his face etched in my memory so as to never forget him. All of a sudden my attention was drawn to two tiny pictures in frames next to his hospital bed. One was of a beautiful woman, his wife, and the other was of four young girls, my sisters and me. The table was bare except for these two tiny frames; both were simple and gold. As I looked at the photos, I knew right then and there that he never forgot us and that he knew we still loved him. The nurse told my dad that Grandpa didn't ask for anything else but to never have those photos removed from his side. All along he had us there with him. We had never left. It's funny how illness and old age can alter the mind, but it can't touch the heart.

valarie Hurtado

Alexandra
Yvonne Flores Lemke

I HAD JUST TURNED THIRTEEN when my mother announced that we would be moving out of the cramped, rat-infested apartment we called home.

The 'rents (a little phrase I coined as early as 1996 referring to my parents) still weren't exactly sure where we would be moving. All we knew at the time was that our rent was going up, so we had two choices. One choice was to move into the new apartments being built beside Stehlik Intermediate. The paint wasn't peeling off the staircases, the wood hadn't turned a rotten black-brown, and the gates weren't bent by middle schoolers—yet.

The other choice, if we could afford it, was to move into a two-story house in Stafford, which, at the time, was pretty much a few isolated roads and antique shops. We had everything packed, but the probability of us actually accomplishing anything, other than boxing up our belongings, still felt pretty slim to me. About a month passed. All talk, no action.

I came home from school one day and attempted to kick open the door, as was my habit, while struggling with my alto saxophone case, exceedingly heavy backpack, and the leftover books that would never fit in the backpack. I had always referred to my kicking open the door as "Bustin' in like the Mafia." I had a thing for violence. The door didn't budge. It was the first time I had encountered a locked door since the first grade, when my mom was late coming home from her friend's house.

I threw my belongings on the ground and, just as I was ready to throw a temper tantrum, Alexandra, my neighbor/best friend, came out of her apartment to call me over.

◆

Alexandra was a year younger than I was. I had known her since she was in the second grade, but we never really got along until one of my friends moved away. It wasn't really Alexandra's having trouble getting along with me, it was my problem with her. I don't quite understand why I chose to dominate and demean her the way I did. It probably had something to do with the first time we had met.

There had been a club I started in third grade with about ten girls from the apartment complex. We basically only told each other secrets and stories, but we had a rule of confidentiality—what was said in the group, stayed in the group. This did not exclude stories of mental, sexual, or physical abuse, which was apparently rampant among our members. The need for privacy was of utmost importance. It was no wonder that I didn't want a parentally attached second grader sneaking around our club premises, which was basically the porch of apartment 232, the one above hers.

"What do you think you're doing?"

She didn't answer. Her dark oversized eyes stared, expressionless.

"What? You can't talk or somethin'?"

No answer. She was starting to creep me out. I grabbed the nearest paper I could, wadded it up, and threw it over the balcony. I never watched the paper fall. I never watched to see if she ran away.

Stupid new girl, I thought.

◆

I trudged uncomfortably to Alexandra's door, trying to balance the books in my right arm, the saxophone in my left hand, and the sliding backpack digging into my right elbow.

"Your mom called," she said, her eyes darting nervously in other directions. "They got the house."

I started muttering curses under my breath while pushing my way into her apartment, the smell of *pupusas* hitting me sharply. I soon shrugged off the anger that was building inside me—maybe I'd be able to finish my seventh grade year at Stovall. I mean, how long could it take to move in, or for us to move out? A month? Two? Three? With all the stuff we had piled up, I wouldn't have been surprised if it had taken years. We didn't even have a truck to help move our couches, bikes, dressers, mattresses, and the kitchen table to name a few things. What about the many boxes of books, toys, and other useless items that were cluttering up the apartment? We could barely get around those.

I spend the rest of the afternoon with Alexandra, refusing to eat . . .

"Lex, you should know by now. I don't eat anything that's not chocolate." Other than those *pupusas*, whose smell permanently tainted the apartment regardless of what was on the stove, I refused to try anything else.

"Sorry."

. . . harassing radio stations . . .

"Hello, this is 104 KRBE—"

"Sorry, we wanted to ask you another question . . . " She twiddles a bit of her cherry-black hair between her fingers.

"Are you the same girls that have called about five times within the last few minutes?"

"Last time, I swear . . . "

. . . and talking about getting married to rock stars . . .

"You know what, Lexy? I'll let you have Gavin Rossdale."

"Really?" Her eyes brighten slightly from their usual darkness.

"Sure . . . I think I wanna marry the lead singer of the Foo Fighters . . . wait . . . what was his name again?"

"I have no idea. I don't even know who the Foo Fighters are."

"That's because you're stupid." I grab the phone. "You call."

"But I called last time! And the last five times!"

My eyes narrow. She picks up the phone.

"Hello?" She laughs nervously. "Yes, it's us—again."

It was about 8 p.m. when the doorbell rang. The 'rents had come for me. My dad's younger sister, Sofia, was bouncing along behind them, unnaturally happy as usual.

"C'mon, Yvonne, you have to help move out your stuff," someone said.

Confused, I asked, "Why? We're not leaving today, are we?"

When they gave me the answer, I started crying. I think that deep down I had really believed that we would never move because we had been too poor to afford anything. I thought, throughout the entire stay at Alexandra's that afternoon, that she had heard wrong—that she was just stupid.

Upset, I made Alexandra walk with me around the apartment complex. The entire time, I passed by trees and poles that would all be victims of both my physical and verbal abuse.

I ended up not helping the 'rents put all our stuff in my aunt's truck. It didn't really matter to them, though—I guess they realized how hard this move was for me.

The moment finally arrived. When my parents waved the signal from Sofia's truck, I knew I was leaving for good. I walked Alexandra back to her door.

"I guess I'm leaving now."

"Yeah."

"I just want to say . . . bye." I kissed her cheek.

She stood in utter shock, as did both of our families, now surrounding us.

My mom tapped me on the shoulder, and I followed her to the truck. I waved at Alexandra. Three years would pass before I'd see her again.

◆

"Lexy?" She is taller than me now.

"Oh my god, Yvonne! How long has it been? Since sixth grade, right?"

"Well, seventh for me. So, I guess it's been three years."

"Right."

She leads me in. We walk upstairs to her bedroom—her new house drenched in the familiar smell of *pupusas*. That's what they call them in El Salvador. I had just found out a few months earlier that Mexicans call them *gorditas*, but I had only tasted them at Alexandra's apartment, so they are *pupusas* to me.

Her little brother Benjamin peeks in at us. Not so little anymore. He still hasn't retired the bowl cut, but he's taller now. He might be about nine.

I wave and smile. He disappears.

Lexy begins to shake slightly. She adjusts her blinds, cleans her room while she speaks, and rearranges her shirt several times.

"Sorry to interrupt, but can I get a drink? Just that I've been thirsty the entire way here."

In the kitchen, she asks if I'm hungry. She is making herself a ham and cheese croissant sandwich.

"Wait a minute, you don't like this . . . do you?"

"I can try it—it looks pretty good."

She looks ecstatic. "Wow, you used to never try anything new, other than my mom's *pupusas.*"

"A lot has changed since I moved. That's why I actually weigh more than seventy-five pounds now." We laugh. As I speak, I see Benjamin peek from the corner. He sees me catch him and hides again.

"Hold up. I've gotta do something," I tell Lexy. "Junior?! Can you come here?!"

Benjamin appears at the doorway. Both Lexy and Benjamin stay completely still. I draw in a breath. "Look—I know in the past I've done things that I shouldn't have *[i have a flashback where i strike junior across the face].* I know I can't take it back *[alexandra tells me to stop],* and I don't condone it *[i push alexandra against the green staircase leading up to apartment*

232], but I—I was messed up. There was something wrong with me. Please forgive me *[she gives me that look]*. I'm not the same person *[it's pain— it's surprise]* that I used to be *[it's terror]*.

The flashback stops. I walk over to hug Junior as Alexandra rushes over to hug me. We grip each other tightly.

Benjamin pulls away. "Do you wanna see our computer?"

"Sure. Hold up, though, lemme finish eating this." I take a bite of the croissant sandwich. "You could go start it up though."

"Okay."

I can feel the house exhale with me.

Befriending Jason

EVERY TIME NINTH GRADE LUNCH ROLLED AROUND, the same thing would happen. Dulles High School was under serious renovations, so we'd stand just outside the cafeteria in the half-built hallway. Todd, who was only 5'3", would talk about his being able to kick so-and-so's ass. Andrew and I would give each other knowing smiles. Everyone would lend me their portable CD players and make me listen to one of the underground hardcore bands that I just "needed to check out." One of Todd's many friends would skip part of their fifth period class, so I would get to meet that person. And whether it was Nigel, Chris, Tom, or Jason, they would all talk about how "messed up" they had been the day before or were going to get the next day. I merely sat on the Sheetrock we weren't allowed to sit on, listening. Amazed. Amused.

I had always been fond of Todd. He had a way of making me feel better than anyone else could. He'd scrunch his eyes as his mouth contorted to form the obscenities that were my vitamins. I was positive he "talked mess" about me too, but it was okay. No one took him seriously anyway.

After a few months of being around my ninth grade lunch group, I gave up my god-given gender and became Todd. I would wear gigantic Jnco's marred with orange-yellow mustard stains (from sandwiches I had dropped weeks before) and a collection of crusty, white spots from each morning's pancake syrup. His objectionable verbs and adjectives appeared in my speech—replacing the ones I had once used. My CD collection began to mirror his collection of the then-underground hardcore bands such as Deftones, Incubus, and Korn as well as other local bands. Our growing similarities did not go unnoticed.

"Do you like Todd?"

"What's *that* s'posed to mean? Of course I like Todd, he's my buddy. But if you're trying to say something else, like I'm *in love* with him or somethin' stupid like that—that's not even right."

Although I attempted to dispel the growing rumor, as well as the one about me being a lesbian, they still circulated. So now I was a lesbian who was so in love with Todd that I'd stalk him. How people believed both of them at the same time, I don't know. I always believed that there was something in the water, targeting everyone with bank accounts large enough to live there—in Sugar Land.

◆

Since Dulles decided to arrange lockers by alphabetical order, my locker was in the then-called "Upstairs A-wing." I had never really paid attention to that fact until one morning before school I saw Jason's long unwashed hair peeking from behind the open locker located about two feet away from mine. *Fickman, Flores, I see.*

"Hey, what's up, Jason?" His hair was probably dirty blonde, but the accumulating grease made it look dark brown in most spots. It was a good thing that I had lost my sense of smell—then again, I'm sure I didn't smell very fragrant myself.

"Nothing." He shoved his books into his locker quickly and said, "I gotta go to class now."

He turned and sped away, leaving me to the emptiness of A-wing.

There were about thirty minutes left before first period.

Kristina, Erika, and Amanda were at my locker the next morning. Any time that they greeted me this way, I would pretend not to be bitter about the fact that Erika and Kristina had been *my* two best friends, the year before.

"Did you talk to Jason yesterday?" Kristina asked.

"Uhh . . . I just said, 'what's up?'"

They all looked at each other.

"What? Did I do something wrong?"

They began to elbow each other, trying to convince each other to tell me.

"Okay. I'm fourteen. I can handle it . . . " More whispers. "Either tell me or don't. I don't really even care—just make up your damn minds whether you're gonna tell me or not."

Amanda showed me a letter that Jason had written to her. In it, he talked about my greeting him and the fact that he thought that the only reason I had even tried to talk to him was because he was friends with Todd. I apparently wasn't capable of making friends with anyone without an ulterior motive.

I scoffed as I read along, but halfway through, I decided to give the letter back to Amanda. Lips pursed. I shook my head, shrugged, and broke away from them.

As I walked to class, I remember that all I could think over and over was how I had just wanted to be able to get along with everyone associated with my new lunch group. And if Jason was able to maintain friendships with those people, whom I knew, even then, were some of the greatest people I would ever meet, then there must've been something inside him worth knowing. That something made him worth befriending.

◆

The summer before tenth grade started, I had a dream about walking into the lunchroom—newly renovated:

I spot Jason and ask where everyone is and he brings me outside. Everyone is sitting at tables around a large fountain. I walk up to my usual lunchtime group. All of the people who were in my ninth grade lunch group and even those in my eighth grade group are sitting together. They all talk about instances that I didn't know had happened — that I would never be able to share because I'm the new girl. Everyone in this town has known each other since elementary school, but I showed up late seventh grade. No one notices when I'm there, and no one notices when I walk away.

◆

It was in the middle of tenth grade. I was sitting on a chalky white bench alone, waiting for Holly and Sylvia to get their lunches. I had known them since the seventh grade, but hadn't really talked to them before, other than a polite sentence or two. I was an outcast now — sitting in the stinging sun, being blinded by the brightened bench.

The guys from my ninth grade lunch group would usually play hacky sack a few feet from where I sat. I would watch longingly but would only greet those who passed by to play. Occasionally someone would talk to me, but it'd usually be Todd introducing me to a new band.

The lunch line must have been long that day, because, along with Holly and Sylvia, the hacky sack group was late.

Jason and Nigel passed by my bench, and I gave a small smile. Jason smirked.

I quickly averted my eyes toward my sandwich bag and started to take out its contents.

"Aww . . . look at the ugly, stupid b—h." By the time I looked up again, he was already kicking the hacky sack toward Nigel.

◆

Fort Bend Independent School District tries to be as outstanding as possible, in the eyes of the state. That year they started a "Youth Conference" during which students nominated by certain teachers get to miss, in total, two full days of school to plan an event. It would be at Wheeler's Field House and would cause district-wide racial awareness.

The school drug counselor, Mrs. Kajandar, nominated me.

◆

I was arguing with myself.

The girl you sat with on the bus on the way to the first Youth Conference isn't here. Paul isn't here either. Which means Jason doesn't have anyone to sit with. Maybe you should . . . no. You don't need him calling you . . . what he did last time. But it can't hurt to try. Yes, it could! You'll get over it. Get up, Yvonne.

I walked over.

"If you want to," Jason shrugged, then leaned back sloppily in his chair, boredom whitewashing his honey-colored eyes.

"Okay then, I will."

Jason stayed with me throughout the entire conference. During someone's long speech on prejudice, we started whispering to each other.

"You see that girl in the red shirt?" He indicates with his eyes.

"The blonde? You think she's hot?"

"Hell yeah! She's in one of my classes . . . "

"Yeah, she's pretty hot."

We spent most of the conference talking about which girls were the hottest at school and which ones were the most attractive at the Youth Conference. The truth is that I was never what the rumors indicated me to be, but sometimes I would use them to my advantage in order to share a male-male bond with my friends—something the "Colgate smile" and "Pantene-haired," Maybelline girls could never do.

Lunch came around and Jason followed me into the lunch area where they had prepared sandwiches for everyone. We walked out of the area, since we were allowed to eat anywhere, and started to head toward the bleachers when some of Jason's friends from Progressive High School invited him outside.

He looked at me and asked, "Do you want to go outside?"

"Whatever you want to do."

He declined. At that moment, I noticed that I had accidentally gotten a chicken salad instead of a chicken sandwich.

I ran back inside the lunch area frantically searching for something ham-less and mayonnaise-less. There were only ham sandwiches and chicken salad left.

Just my luck. And I was sure Jason would be gone by the time I got out of the area.

When I finally rushed out, I found him leaning lightly against a handrail holding the Styrofoam box, facing the direction of the door I had run through.

"You find it?"

"No, but I guess I'll just try to wipe off the mayonnaise. I hate mayonnaise."

"Hell yeah, that stuff is nasty."

◆

At the end of the day, the people at the Youth Conference gave everyone a package of Big Red. The object: Give five people a stick of gum and "make a friend." Of course, Jason used this as an opportunity to hit on one of the girls we had been talking about earlier, but she ignored him.

"Aww . . . she doesn't want to be my friend."

He leaned his head on my shoulder for faux-comfort and I gave him his faux-sympathy.

"Aww . . . well, you don't need her. I'll be your friend."

He picked his head up and looked at me, lifting his eyebrows. "Really?"

And we exchanged gum.

Leaving
Marisol León

I AM 3,000 MILES AWAY FROM HOME . . . and I love it. I love the snow, and the gray sky, and everything about my new life. Because for the first time in my life—my life—I can live for myself. I can choose. I can breathe. I call the shots.

Mi tío Chuy me apodó "Chapetes." Otros "Cachetona" o "Chata." Mi abuelito me decía "el diablito."

Me llamo Marisol. Pero para mis padres y para mis amigos simplemente soy Mari.

Mari. La traviesa. Pinche Mari.

I never thought I would come this far. I mean, never in my wildest dreams. All I wanted was to get out of my house. I didn't understand why my parents acted the way they did, why they said the things they said: *"Nomás no la vayas a regar, Mari." "Con ese humor, no habrá hombre que te aguante."* So, I couldn't wait to take off.

And I did.

Mis padres nacieron en Degollado, Jalisco, México. Ambos crecieron en casitas sin luz y sin agua. Mi amá apenas sabe leer y escribir, y mi apá nunca terminó la secundaria. Él se vino pa'l otro lado cuando tenía diecisiete años. Después de juntar dinero (trabajando en un hospital como cocinero, donde todavía trabaja después de treinta años), mandó a pedir por mi mamá, y ella dejó todo:— sus padres, hermanos, amigos pa' venirse con él.

Although my parents emigrated to the United States thirty years ago from Mexico, they raised me and my sister the way they knew best: *a lo mexicano*. Growing up, I wore the dresses my mother made for me; my parents continuously emphasized the importance of learning how to be a good "housewife"; and I wasn't allowed to sleep over at friends' houses, let alone date or have a boyfriend.

As I grew older, my parents began to question my priorities. Rather than be delighted with my grades, they wondered why I didn't dedicate more time to cooking and cleaning. Early, I realized my parents and I belong to two separate worlds. I am an urban twenty-first-century female, and my parents grew up in a nineteenth-century-like agrarian society. We never discussed the books I read (we never had books in our house while growing up), or the friends I had, or the projects I undertook.

Yo . . . yo nací en Los Ángeles, California. Soy méxicoamericana. Chicana.

Nunca comprendí por qué mi madre siempre estaba de mal humor. No fue hasta hace poco que llegué a entenderlo. Ella no tiene amigas ni amigos. Se la pasa todo el día limpiando. Y pa' acabarla, también trabaja. Y nunca recibió de mi padre la atención ni el afecto que ella necesitaba. Mi padre, el típico machista, no la dejaba salir.

Both of my parents live confined to a different set of walls. My mother does not speak English and does not know how to drive. So she stays at home most of the time, keeping in touch with her family through phone conversations. My father has worked at the same place since he arrived in the States and has little or no hope of ever being able to pursue his passion for writing and music.

Sé que han llegado a ser muy infelices. Llenos de sueños que nunca realizaron. De anhelos, de antojos . . .

They never thought I would leave. I remember Tía Olivia calling the house to let me know I was betraying my family by leaving to study. But unlike both of my parents, I wasn't leaving the country to let years pass before seeing my family again; and unlike my mother, I wasn't leaving to get married. I told Tía Olivia that, but she refused to understand.

Still, it worked out for the best. I never expected my parents and I to become this close as a result of my parting. My dad and I have always been friends, but now he doesn't worry about me as much. I actually think he has newfound trust and *respect* for me. This past year he started writing me letters—beautiful letters—in which he articulates feelings and frustrations about work, family, and life that I never thought he would be willing or able to share.

And my mom . . . we had a talk a while back and things seem to be working out. Finally, we talk about my friends—she knows their names! And she recently asked: *"¿Y qué dicen los muchachos? ¿Ya tienes novio?"* But what I treasure the most are the messages she leaves on my voice mail—messages that I replay when I get homesick and find comfort in . . . even though they always make me wish that my leaving had not been what, in the end, brought us closer.

Through leaving, I have come to experience a whirlwind of feelings and emotions—I've felt guilty, proud, empowered, and even depressed at times. *Y por eso yo . . . yo no me voy a quedar con las ganas. He venido tan lejos para seguir y realizar mis sueños. Yo sé que mis padres no pudieron por las circunstancias —pero yo no tengo ninguna excusa. Aquí, tengo el privilegio de hasta escoger cuáles clases quiero tomar, que si quiero ser arquitecta, doctora, abogada— cualquier cosa. Y yo . . . yo quiero escribir.* I want to provide a voice for the Latina . . . for all Latinos. I want to educate, increase awareness, affect change in my community through my writing. . . . I want to succeed—not just for myself or my parents. *Por y para la raza.* And of course, I want independence. In every sense of the word. I don't ever want my happiness, my mobility, my strength to depend on anyone or anything. *¿Yo? Ya parece.*

I am a Yale Chicana. Struggling to make ends meet and all the while never forgetting where I come from. My heart is, and always will be, in *Los Ángeles.* I look back . . . and I smile. *Porque sé que aunque estoy lejos . . . siempre los mantengo muy cerquita de mí, aquí en mi corazón.* My family. The people who taught me how to speak, how to write. . . how to take pride in the fact *que por mis venas corre sangre cien por ciento mexicana.*

Algún día regresaré a Los Ángeles ya pa' quedarme allí. Pero antes voy a seguir viviendo una vida que mis padres nunca pudieron vivir. I am the product of their hard labor, of their sacrifices and unfulfilled dreams. And as I look back at the fights, arguments, and compromises, I feel nothing but blessed for their leaving and mine.

unforgettable friend
flor lopez

"JUST A BOY, just an ordinary boy trying to get by . . . " I sang the lyrics of the song in front of the mirror one Friday night as I made my way through the kitchen, listening to my silvery-grayish oval boom box. Usually people go out this day, but not me. I am the exception to the rule. I have homework and exams to prepare for—giving up my social life, for the desired academic success. I wish I would receive surprises in my life, but my life as a student is too plain and ordinary for that.

Oh well, I have to go back and focus my attention on my research project.

"Riinnnnnggggg!!!!" I tried to ignore the ring as I went back to my desk.

"Flor, the phone is ringing!!" said my mother, watching her favorite movie on television.

"It's for you . . . " She said as she handed the phone to me.

"Who is it, Mami?" I asked.

Who could be calling me so late? It was almost midnight. No way—everyone knows better!

"There is a boy on the line; his name is Jesús. He says he wants to speak to you; he sounds very sweet and polite. He might be one of your classmates," she reassured me. I could not possibly think who was on the other end of the line.

"Hello?" I said.

"Hey!" a voice answered with excitement on the other end.

"Who is this?" I asked with a frown on my face.

"Ooh . . . have you forgotten about me?" It was more of a statement than a question.

I was shocked! I had not heard that voice in one year. It was my "old" best friend, Jesse. But because time had passed and distance separated us, the term "best friend" did not apply to him as before. Nine years had passed without seeing him. Why had he called after so long?

♦

It was the beginning of eighth grade, an exciting school year to make new friends and feel "cool" for being an upperclassman. I had been at the same school for three years, since sixth grade, therefore knowing people was not a problem. However, I still did not know the entire school like I unrealistically planned in seventh grade. It was a goal impossible to achieve.

There were different groups in middle school, just like high school. There was the "cool crowd" who usually wore preppy clothes (maybe Tommy Hilfiger, if they were lucky). There were the gangsters or, in slang terms, "O.G.s" and "wannabes," who mostly wore Dickies that showed their boxers, with pants all the way to the bottom of their shoes, with tons of Blue Magic hair gel for their wet look, talking with their hand gestures as they managed to do the sleek cat walk across the hallways. On the other hand, the "jocks" were usually good-looking with a great body posture and build. They might not be too smart at times, but they did have exceptional people skills as they managed to talk to all the girls in the lunchroom. Last but not least, we had the "nerds" along with the "Goths." They were not always seen, but always on the dark side of the spectrum. They hung outside of school, by the dark halls or by the library, usually by the art and drama classes. The "nerds" were always seen playing chess at their tournaments in the computer science classrooms. Everyone was interesting; the school was diverse and full of flavor; I had a mixture of every flavor; I didn't belong in any one group.

I had a group of friends who also did not need to belong or fit in. We mostly had met the previous year. Some of us had just reunited in English class to form stronger bonds and live significant experiences together. We hung out during lunch, talked, laughed, played, and sometimes fought. We all had our little issues at times. We talked to the popular kids without feeling inferior, but we knew we did not belong there. We even talked to seventh graders, as well as all the different group members. Five boys and eight girls composed my group of close friends.

I thought of my male friends as immature but funny, nice, clever, and street smart. There were many, but three of them were the closest. There was José or "Shorty." He was the biggest clown, the smooth talker in our group; he was charismatic and drew attention with his humble yet flirtatious personality, cute with a vivacious look in his eyes. Yet, he was too immature and would always get into trouble in class by throwing paper airplanes.

On the other hand there was Israel. He looked like Tigger from Winnie the Pooh, with long ears and a big nose. He was funny in a childlike way, innocent, and naïve. He never got into trouble. He was sweet and liked to whistle. He would always watch after me. My third and future best friend was yet unknown to me.

◆

This is how we met.

He was sitting down by the edge of the black wooden table, white paper and sharpened yellow No. 2 pencil in his hand, drawing lines and contours of what constituted part of his creation, a lowrider car surrounded with velvet red roses.

As I entered the white-lighted room of my science class, I noticed his athletic silhouette and well-developed height for a fourteen-year-old boy, casting a lean shadow by the window of the science lab. He looked at me through the corner of his eyeglasses, giving rise to a smart, quiet, intellectual look mixed with a thuggish style indicated by how he wore his black baggy

Jinkles. He had a cute smile, with dimples when he laughed. I noticed a white line of perfect mother-of-pearl teeth, contrasting with the rosy complexion of his lips. He was already known to me as JZ, short for his name.

His hair was combed back, straight and sleek, giving a shiny appearance as he wore gel to accentuate the dark color of his midnight black hair, emphasizing the light café au lait of his complexion.

"I have you for English, right? My name is JZ . . . what's yours?" he said approaching me as he left his masterpiece behind. I smelled his cologne, fresh and vigorous like his persona. Boy, he was cute but arrogant.

"You draw pretty good, but I can show you how to draw better," I said blushing and giggling. He looked at me with a puzzled look on his face, not expecting a challenge as an introduction.

This was the beginning of my friendship with JZ. A fight to see who did better, a challenge for both of us because it implied an opportunity to beat each other, and at the end we both would always end up winning somehow. It might have been competition, but we both knew deep inside that each of us was as good as the other. We had the opportunity to grow and learn from each other. It was a weird but fun encouragement to do our best.

Throughout the years we were friends, I discovered JZ was a reserved guy. He was also the leader of his friends, the protector, the guy who would not fight unless he had to defend himself or others. He was honest with respect to himself and everyone, sensitive with a big heart, a poet and a philosopher with a deep perspective on life. You could always see him drawing with his paper notebook and yellow half-worn pencil in his hand, always showing beauty. The undiscovered artist, yet daring like no one else. Respected by the O.G. crowd, he played chess with the nerds and lost at checkers with me. Bouncing like a ball, high then low, when he bounced low all of a sudden he would manage to rise high. That was JZ. He would never give up; he would never give up with me.

We would speak for hours on the telephone, sometimes about deep subjects like life or philosophy, sometimes about silly stuff that teenagers talk about. Sometimes long pauses of silence made up the conversation. People would see us playing basketball together, as I managed to steal the ball from that rough guy. He was my best friend, almost a brother to me. I possibly found him attractive at times, but it was his approach to life that I found extraordinarily inspiring, regardless of his troubled brothers. It was his love for art and his mother that kept him going.

◆

We spoke, but he was no longer the same person I once knew. Time had passed. I guess too much time changes people's dreams and expectations.

He said he was running away from the law. I was shocked to hear this. I didn't want to ask why.

He said he owed people money. Where were the goals and objectives he had when we were kids?

He told me he had run away from home trying to prove himself, trying to be a self-made man, but finally had to go back to his mother. He could not make it out on the streets.

"Life is too tough out there . . . please, be somebody. Please pursue a brighter future," he urged me.

"What about *your* future?" I asked.

"I'll be okay. I know what I'm doing. It's about time, you see . . . I leave everything for the last minute, remember when we were in school?"

"But this is not school anymore, this is life, JZ. You used to say 'Knowledge is power.' Well, where is *your* knowledge? Where is *your* power?"

I only heard silence on the other end.

Years had passed, and I didn't know much about him. We went to different high schools. I became the nerd, and he became the gangster; we lost touch. I only know what he wanted to say. I only heard what I didn't want to hear.

Flor Lopez

Men Also Cry

Juan Macias

THERE WAS A POINT IN MY LIFE when I believed men couldn't cry. I was just a child and had reached the age at which hopes of becoming Superman fade away, allowing images of one's father to infiltrate the mind in their place. Unfortunately, my dad was like every other man in Mexico, bitter and hardened by decades of self-imposed ideas of machismo. Although he roundly denied it, I believe in his subconscious lay the fear of being singled out by friends and relatives for expressing his feelings openly. It was unheard of for a man to commit social suicide by simply manifesting this weakness associated only with the opposite sex. This story captures my first steps toward becoming an ordinary macho man and my journey into a world of new feelings.

It is ironic to suggest that my mother was the one to exhort my commencement in machismo, but it is true. As more people became fascinated with my mature character as a child, my mother's pride rose higher. "What a brave and serious boy you have, Marilú," friends and relatives commented frequently. "Can you believe he is only six years old?" my mother's response always came in a lofty tone. Her radiant smile made butterflies fill my stomach. Just as every son hopes to please his mother, I wished for her to receive nothing less than satisfaction from me. Considering the great results from emulating my father's personality, I decided to take it to the next level.

However, my father had an amazing individuality that proved hard to imitate. He was an honest man and a diligent electrician, who managed to keep every section of his life in perfect order. One of my father's most obvious characteristics was his unflinching nature. This gave him an impressive ability to suppress fear. At the age of six I was very observant of his unique capabilities and attempted to mimic them whenever an opportunity presented itself. It wasn't long before the fear of dark and concealed places died away. Even when power failures occurred and every other boy trembled under his mother's hug, I managed to go on with my business normally. Being more like my father also brought me new responsibilities. He was not a man who took pleasure in killing time. It was only because of him that everything in our house with screws and wires worked. I began to make myself useful as much as I could at that age. Both of my parents were very proud when they noticed that their son didn't have to be told what to do, that he had the ability to do everything on his own. Simple chores, such as maintaining an impeccable room and taking out the trash, brought joy to them, which made me happy also.

This phase of taking in everything around me and emulating it brought me to the impression that machismo was the only respectable way of life for men. There was no margin for anything else because this idea suffocated my existence from every angle. Soon I began to examine my father's many brothers as well as close family friends. Similarities among all of them were evident concerning both personality and traits. At times in my childhood I wondered if there were more boys like me in the world, who observed adults in order to grow up fast.

Both of my parents suffered greatly as they kept their troubles hidden from my sister and I. They awarded themselves only brief moments late at night, once we had been put to sleep, to discuss them. I never heard them arguing, but I suspected something was definitely wrong because the living room's light could be seen through the crack underneath our door. Although my developing macho character urged my indifference and to keep out of curiosity's way, one day I asked my mother to explain what was happening. She didn't tell me right away. Instead she looked into my eyes as if she was examining my very conscience. The proud feeling of being trusted was quickly overpowered by the brusque fear caused by what she said. My mother explained that for years our family had been very fortunate to evade every danger, but now it found itself pinned between the two great moving forces of hunger and fear. Even a young and innocent mind like mine understood how several epochs of corrupt leaders in addition to an apathetic society had sunk my country into an economic turmoil.

Slowly but surely, miserable conditions began to take the reins of our lives. I myself suffered from many sleepless nights. The thin, jagged line of light from under my door continued to stir my curiosity, but I dared not ask anything of their new discussions. Sometimes my mother lost control and began to cry, loud enough for me to feel her pain. My father would turn off the light and direct her to their room as soon as this happened. Three long weeks passed before my father devised a drastic solution that would completely change my family's life forever.

I remember that day well. My mother picked up my sister and me from the school just around the corner from our home. As I opened the door, I caught a glimpse of my father sitting at the huge, dark, wooden table with a blank stare. Moments later my mother was beside him holding his left hand in hers. It was awkward to be standing before our father at that time of the day, knowing that he wasn't expected home from work until a much later time. Mother spoke first, responding to my little sister's impatient sigh. She explained to her all that I already knew. Father's formidable voice came next, slashing through my sister's crying. He continued to speak but in a different tone now, much more delicate. I could have sworn I heard a crack in his voice as he expressed his plan to immigrate to the United States in hopes of providing a better life for us.

Two days later, we were in our yellow Volkswagen heading toward the Central de autobuses downtown. I admired my father's concentration on the road straight ahead. That day he had not looked in the eyes of anyone in our family. In the passenger seat my mother wore a long face and slowly wiped the tears crawling down her red cheeks. I was the only one truly maintaining self-control. My sister beside me hung on to my shoulder crying and sobbing, imploring me to act. The car came to an abrupt stop, breaking the monotony of the night. My father told us to act natural, and then he walked ten feet in front of us, still dodging our saddened looks.

We were late, as we were to every place, and the departure of my father's bus was announced through the loudspeakers moments after we entered. "They're boarding already!" my father yelled and began to run without turning his body more than halfway toward us.

I never saw my father get on that bus. I did, however, catch a glimpse of him pressing his face against the cold bus window. His warm breath fogged the glass, making it almost impossible to see anything inside. I squinted as the bus drove near me toward the exit of the bus depot just before it lost itself in the city's busy streets. His window passed no more than four feet away from me. There he was, looking down at the family he was forced to leave in order to offer us a better chance in life. The tears that inundated his eyes suddenly fell upon his face and distorted his sharp features. He stared down into nothing, with his hands pressed against the glass as a prisoner shows his impotence days before his execution.

This image will remain with me forever. It reminds me of my father's sacrifice and how much he loves me and all of his family. But it also reminds me of how much I love him, for I cried just as much as he did.

In that moment I came to realize that the true heart of the machismo life exists only as an illusion. No man on the face of the earth could have repressed the sentiments my father experienced that night. Even the most macho man never ceases to feel, but rather puts on a cold and bitter mask to hide that which is so essential to the being, our emotions. In that moment of enlightenment, my emerging macho life ventured into a world of new feelings. A world in which I can finally become a complete and authentic man who isn't afraid any longer to take advantage of every pleasure in life.

The first

Annette Teresa Martinez

I SAT ON THE EDGE OF HIS TWIN BED, pretending to watch "Reservoir Dogs," wishing the hours until my ten-thirty curfew would come faster. Wishing I had chosen not to skip art class and use my last dollar to take the Metro bus over here. If only I had met a nice lacrosse-playing white boy from school, one with a car. But I didn't. And I didn't exist in their world, anymore than they existed in mine, though I had been "visiting" their honors classes the last four years of high school. Besides I was determined to keep it real even though I didn't speak Spanish or grow up with my mom making homemade tortillas every morning. No, I think it was the fact that I was one of three Hispanic girls in the honors program at the school on the other side of the working class and knowing that even the teachers merely referred to us collectively as "the little brown girls" that made me determined to embrace my brownness; brownness that made me stand out, but still be mostly invisible.

The arch in my back began to tighten as if someone were twisting a screwdriver in it.

"Why don't you lay back here with me?"

"No thanks, I'm fine." The sound of his itchy voice pushed me further toward the edge at the foot of the bed and away from him. I didn't want to turn around and look at him with his back resting against the headboard, pale brown arms crossed behind his head, and his hairless chest stretched out like an accordion. Shifting back my weight to rest upon my palms, I felt tiny, hard grains of sand from the sheets slip through my fingertips and become trapped underneath my fingernails. I was disgusted. I was disgusted by his lack of concern for cleanliness. But I was more disgusted at myself for allowing him to deem me no longer worth the effort.

Then, just at that very moment—almost as if he could feel my thoughts, which I often believed he could—he lowered his arm in the most tender of gestures as he cautiously put down the lukewarm can of Budweiser, which he had bravely stolen from the fridge when his father was not looking. I watched from the corner of my eye, the tiny droplets dancing around the can in a kamikaze downward spiral to the unvarnished floor that was rotting away. He walked over to open the door of his bedroom, which led to the backyard.

The three o'clock afternoon sun burst through the door like police on a raid. At first, I welcomed its illumination, but seconds later, I found myself falling back into the shadows of embarrassment with the feeling that someone would catch me here; fearful that it would be my parents. I could be in art class right now, sculpting with clay and guilt-free. But instead, I was here with him and feeling shamed that he would stand there on the broken concrete steps, waving his dick around and pissing where anyone might see. He turned to me and gave me his snarly smile, proud at his own ability to drink so much and not have to urinate until that moment.

He wasn't beautiful with a chiseled jaw like Seneca, the cute skater from Algebra 2. And he definitely wasn't charming, but then again when you're sweet seventeen and never been kissed, charm is not exactly what you are looking for, especially when even the boys in ESL prefer the 5'7" blondes in the Cole Haan loafers. Those River Oaks and West U blondes with the Dooney and Burke leather bags were as common as the brand-new SUV's that lined the student parking lot. Yet, the ginger-skinned boys with their faded flannel shirts never tired of blowing through loosely clenched teeth, making that "chit, chit" sound whenever those girls walked by.

"This feels so fuckin' great. You know what would make this even more better . . . a big fat blunt. Hand me my Zippo, would 'ya?"

His faded linen slacks with the perfect creases lay thrown by my feet. The pockets were worn thin by his free-floating worldly possessions—a pack of filterless Camel cigarettes, a pack of Zig-Zags, two sticks of Wrigley's winterfresh gum, and his good-luck charm, a purple amethyst stone. I remember the day when he told me that purple was his favorite color because it represented royalty. I leaned over to pull the tarnished brass lighter from the pocket whose seams were on the verge of giving way under its weight. These pockets would have to be mended soon, but I doubted he would ever make that much of an effort. Someone once told me that a woman could be judged by the items she carries in her purse. I wondered if the same could also apply to a man and his wallet. But he didn't carry a wallet or even a Texas ID. He was waiting for his eighteenth birthday when all his records would be cleared.

Against my wishes, my gaze followed as the sunlight reflected directly on the bedroom walls where the paint was almost nonexistent. As I read the bleeding poetic quotes of Jim Morrison and Ozzie Osborne that he had carved into them, I tried to drown out the sound of his smoky cough. Along with his scratchy howl of laughter, it was as pleasant to my senses as the wailing of cats in heat. I used to find him deep and thought-provoking, but now I realized he was just disturbed. But still I was not ready to walk away. I felt obligated out of pity and, despite everything, a little bit special. Special and flattered that the high school dropout with the shiny Stacy Adams shoes had chosen me from all the other girls who I worked with at the theater. Girls with smooth and easy straight black hair, faces adorned with drugstore cosmetics and eyebrows shaped like an S. Girls that had probably been kissed many times before and would be many times after. Yet it was my small, unpolished hand that he held in his when the lights went out and all the people were seated. His fingers, long like spoons dipped in chocolate pudding, tickling my palms as we spoke of nothing and everything all at once.

"I love this part, where the guy cuts off the other mother-fucker's ear. He's one bad son of a bitch. What's wrong with you?"

"Nothing's wrong with me."

"I know what's wrong with you. You need some of this herb! Come on, take a hit."

"No thanks. I don't want any."

"You never wanna smoke out with me. It's cool, though. I like that. You have class. Plus, I don't have to worry about you smokin' up all my crop. I remember I used to mess with this one girl, always beggin' me for my weed. Her name was Tina. She used to be so fine. But you're prettier than her, she looks like a crackhead now."

There's not much anyone can say after a compliment like that.

And so I said nothing. Nothing that day or the next, just like in school when the teachers called me Cynthia or Anita without even looking in my direction. I remained silent, just as I had when one of those silky boys from English class asked me who this Selena person was who had gotten shot and killed last month. And even if I had something to say, they wouldn't have heard me anyway. The sound of my voice didn't work in their golden-haired, peachy-skinned world, yet it didn't seem to fit in my real world of brown either.

Glamour

Rosaura L. Martinez

MY SOPHOMORE YEAR at Stafford High School was one of many changes. It led me from one group of friends, to none, to another. It was at this point I decided to do something different, like playing sports. Why I waited so far along in school, I'll never know. The only sport I sort of knew how to play was volleyball. My freshmen P.E. class was held across the gym from where the girl's volleyball team practiced. Peeking, I would try memorizing techniques to use later at tryouts. Being part of the team wasn't easy; tryouts were very competitive and usually biased since the girls who had made the team the year before were almost guaranteed a spot in the upcoming year. Unfortunately, I missed tryouts my sophomore year due to missing the information given out while I was out of town for summer vacation. However, I wasn't ready to give up; I just couldn't put my dream to sleep. The plastic, rubber smell of the gym, the noise of a hundred balls bouncing off the brick walls, the laughter and joy that was created by the players when someone messed up—I wanted to be a part of all of it. Being one of the popular girls on the team seemed more attractive than the actual sport.

The first thing I decided was that it was important to meet the girls. Because they played volleyball, they always portrayed an image of toughness and seemed stuck-up. A few of them were in my classes. This is how I got to be a part of their "clique" or, at least, that's what I thought.

Denisse and Jackie proved my image wrong. They sat close to me in English class during the fall semester of our sophomore year. Both had dirty-blonde hair, wore the latest fashions (tight hip jeans with big brand names on their shirts), and the Tommy Girl Freedom perfume. Our "friendship" started when they asked if they could play with my long hair. After a while it became a habit, and I remember leaving class with a new hair-do every day. Later we started talking about boys, shoes, and things I wasn't interested in at the time but came to love during our conversations. Sometimes after school we would hang out around the gym, and they would teach me some moves to use in the upcoming tryouts. They were my coaches for volleyball, not only warning me of mistakes on the court but also about a girl called Sarah. Everyone talked trash about her behind her back. I never really understood why since I didn't get the chance to get to know her. So, I never really had proof that anything people said about her was true. All I can remember is looking over my shoulder at lunchtime, when I would hear a loud (almost fake) laugh coming from across the cafeteria. I would soon spot Sarah bobbing her head back, opening her mouth wide with laughter.

Then there was Janet, who always comes to mind with a single image: As I pull out my picture from the container full of the liquid used to develop film (which smelled like sausage), Janet hands me a towel to dry my hands as I grab my photograph. She was a "tomboy." In my opinion, the best player on the team. She was a senior so she had more experience. She already had three recruiters trying to take her to A&M, UH, and SFA. She was a positive thinker and very laid back; she also gave great advice. Too bad we met during her last year of high school.

All these girls were great and unique in their own ways, honestly, and it's not that I used the girls because I wanted in. Even though our friendship was not thoroughly sincere on my part, I wanted to at least have something to fall back on in case I didn't make the team the next year. Throughout the year I grew even more anxious for August to come, and I practiced almost every day after school. I was so ready for tryouts by January, and then I met Thanh.

Thanh portrayed an image of toughness mixed with wildness and sprinkled with beauty: a beautiful rebel. She had short black hair, thick lips, and brown eyes behind gray contact lenses. A belly-button piercing and a unique symbol tattooed on her lower back. She was the rebel of the team. I would say the smartest one too, since she used her popularity to attract guys and have them please her every demand. This included paying for her lunch, giving her money for a kiss, and even getting the answer sheet to a test she hadn't studied for. We met during our sophomore spring semester in art class. She always walked in with a smell of Cool Water perfume mixed with cigarette smoke. Thanh was the kind of person my parents would've never let me hang out with—she didn't care what people thought about her. Ambitious and not easy to knock out in any way—physically or emotionally. I saw her as a fighter, struggling through anything that blocked her path; she was my idol for a long time. I thought she was invincible, and I took it upon myself to be like her. That is, until Jason came along.

He was the typical "ladies' man," who played around with girls' feelings just to see what he could get out of them. He was one of my closest friends but after what happened with Thanh, everything changed. They went out for a while, maybe three months; she walked in on him and another girl. Then he asked her to join them, and laughed. She came to my house that night, and somehow the image of toughness drained away while I saw her crying. Her mascara ran down her cheeks, making the white tissue in her hands turn black. She was depressed for a long time after that; her entire personality changed. She was quiet and even missed a couple of volleyball games, but somehow we stuck together and made it through. Out of all the girls on the team, I always felt closer to Thanh. We learned from each other and realized that our lives could not depend on one thing all the time. She made me understand that no matter how popular you are, there is only you inside all that glamour.

I didn't try out the following year. I was quite prepared for it, but I realized that even though I had made new friends, they were not what I was looking for. In a way I was relieved I didn't try out. After I met most of the girls, I realized that I had been more blinded by the glamorous sight of being popular than by the game itself. Now that I look back at the different experiences I had with these girls, it makes me wonder why I even wanted to be part of the team in the first place. Popularity, glamour, that's all it was in high school. When you're young, it's a big deal. Is it really worth it? It sure feels like it at the time. Unfortunately, it's all glamour. Not everything that shines is gold, and not everything in a volleyball team has to do with volleyball.

Matsuharu's Quest
Victor Matsumura

I REMEMBER THE FIRST TIME my father told me the story. We were sitting at the dining table in our usual spots with our dirty dishes in front of us. I must have been about twenty, and there was no one else in our middle-class, two-story house on this occasion. We began to talk as we always do after dinner, telling stories about what happened at work or school. Sometimes we even debate history, religion, and politics. This time our discussions somehow led us to the subject of my grandfather. It's unbelievable how one subject can lead to another without anyone really noticing. "Your grandpa was really something," my father told me with a hint of nostalgia in his voice. I never met my grandfather, but from what I hear, he must have really been something.

◆

According to my family's story, Matsuharu Matsumura was born in 1906 to a family of poor Catholic workers in Japan. No one is sure what they did for a living. But he didn't have a bright future and his parents knew it. He went to school, but it still would have been very difficult for him to be successful in Japan. When Matsuharu turned twenty, he was given an opportunity he could not pass up. He could leave Japan in a voyage that would last three months by boat and go to either Mexico or the United States. His father offered him some money he'd saved throughout his life and combined them with Matsuharu's life savings. After thinking about it, Matsuharu decided that Mexico was where he wanted to go. No one is really sure why he chose Mexico over the United States. I guess it was a leap of faith.

He had to leave everything behind. It's tough to have to depart from your home, family, friends, and culture to start all over by yourself. Every immigrant knows exactly how that is. I know exactly how that is—coming to the United States from Mexico City when I was six was the hardest thing I have ever done.

As far as I know, he never spoke about what happened during the three-month trip across the Pacific Ocean. Matsuharu arrived in the state of Colima, located between Jalisco and Michoacán, with a bag of clothes and one hundred dollars. Taking all of their possessions, he and a few other Japanese immigrants decided that they would find a place to live together and share the bills. After a few days, he decided to invest in merchandise consisting of string, buttons, sewing needles, combs, and brushes. He would sell these items out on the street and earn some money for his food and rent.

For about two years Matsuharu spread out sheets of newspaper and laid them out on the sidewalk along with his merchandise. He usually sold to people from the Japanese community, but when Mexican customers stopped by, it was hard for him to communicate with them. The use of body language and broken Spanish was essential for him. The frustrations he had to go through, not being able to decipher what people were asking, must have been terrible. I know from my own experience of leaving Mexico for the United States that it's not easy learning a necessary second language. The difference is that at least my family was with me.

As people walked by, all he could do was sit on the dirty pavement and wait for someone to read the price and buy one of the items. When he was lucky, he picked up a few Spanish words from his customers that he used every time he could. Little by little he learned enough to come up with phrases and some sentences of his own. I am sure he derived a little satisfaction and self-motivation from this.

After thinking about it, Matsuharu decided to go to Mexico City. He was getting nowhere in Colima, and it was time for a change. He packed all his meager possessions and said good-bye to the people he had befriended. He walked to the train station, and he was on his way to the capital of Mexico.

Mexico City was not all that different from Colima for Matsuharu. In fact, except for the larger amount of people found in the capital, his life didn't change at all. Still living in the poverty he just could not shake off, Matsuharu was again selling his same merchandise out on the streets. He did try to get some sort of secure employment, but no one would hire a hardworking Japanese man when they could hire a fluent Spanish speaker. It just wasn't good for business.

Frustration rising again and again was something he could not avoid. Not one soul would give him a chance to prove himself worthy of regular employment. For years and years he tried to learn as much Spanish as he could, but it was all for nothing. He wasn't given a second thought. He was a Japanese with an accent, therefore not hireable. I would have thought this would devastate any man, but not him. He would not go down. Not even after twenty more years of his life.

Twenty years is a very long time. It was for that long that Matsuharu lived in Mexico before he decided to go to college. UNAM (Universidad Nacional Autónoma de México) would be his school for the next five years. He majored in dentistry under the name of Roberto Matsumura. No one knows why he chose that major or that first name. He just did what he did and that was the end of it. No one had the right to ask him why.

He was done with his academic education at the age of forty-five. Roberto Matsumura was a certified dentist.

Roberto rented a place he turned into a clinic in Colonia Guerrero, a poor neighborhood in Mexico City that gets worse and worse as time goes by. Now graffiti is sprayed all over the walls and people have more than one lock on all of their doors. It's the type of place where people have to pay the local criminals and corrupt cops for "protection."

He used the same materials he had left over from his classes at the university. As more customers came in and word about him got around the neighborhood, the better materials he could invest in. All of his money went into the clinic, and he found himself homeless again. He earned his bread and butter in that clinic and that's where he ate, slept, bathed, and did everything we all do in our homes.

After some time he was finally able to buy his own house and send money back to his family during World War II. He would even wear a suit every day. Matsuharu was never poor again.

◆

My grandfather was a rock. No, a boulder. Unmovable and determined.

Looking at his pictures, I can see the hardships in his eyes. In every photo he wears a dark-colored suit and tie. His hair is well-groomed and his face is shaved clean. He looks straight out at me through his large framed glasses from the black-and-white prints. I guess my grandfather was always looking forward. I can see how from picture to picture he gets older and looks more tired, but he looks forward.

To this day, I don't understand why he chose the path he did. While many others gave up after only a few years, he didn't. He stayed in Mexico and fought his way through a miserable life to one of success. Some people might think that he did all this for survival. I think he did it because he would not take no for an answer.

Every time I feel frustrated or depressed or both, I think about how lucky I am to have everything I need. Compared to him, I have always lived in paradise. He went through hell for his children and his children's children. Sometimes I take that for granted. I know for a fact that I am not, nor will ever be, the man my grandfather was.

The Dreaded Piano
Gabriel Medina

THE DREADED PIANO SAT IN FRONT OF ME. I looked at what time it was to make sure that I didn't go longer than the minimum thirty minutes. I was eight years old and practicing the piano was a chore. My dad made me do it every day. Worse than practicing was going to those damn concerts. Putting on those tight shoes that gave me blisters and the clip-on tie that suffocated me was torture.

I was dressed and ready to go in my usual concert outfit of blue slacks, a dress shirt, clip-on tie, a jacket, and dress shoes. Our seats were high—which was normal when we went to concerts—so we had to climb at least five long flights of stairs before sitting down. My dad had gotten tickets to a piano concert that night. Some Russian—Yevgeny Kissin—was the performer. My dad had told the family that Kissin was supposed to be amazing, but they were always the same to me. I had never stayed awake past intermission.

The concert began. It was an all-Chopin program ranging from nocturnes, his famous "Eroica" polonaise, to his extremely famous "Funeral March" sonata. Kissin, the pianist, with his large Afro haircut and a six-feet-four-inch body frame, took his seat on the bench and began playing. The sonata spewed from his fingers and the notes haunted the air with their tragic sounds. I recognized the third movement, the "Funeral March," for its common use in cartoons whenever someone dies. The pianist brought a feeling of melancholy to his audience, and it seemed as if he had, in fact, lost a close friend or a family member.

125

It was this exact moment when I realized that playing the piano is not only about playing the right notes. The piano is about telling a story. It is a means of expression that can be used during our modern age when people are laughed at or criticized for expressing what they truly feel. I myself am somewhat of a shy person; it can be hard for me to express what I feel, whether it is anger, sadness, or sometimes even happiness. The piano is what allows me to share these feelings without any hesitation or timidness.

The next piece was completely different in sound as well as in its message. The "Eroica" polonaise is a piece that can only be performed well by a true virtuoso, such as Kissin, because of its rapid jumps and octaves. The polonaise got its nickname from its large, strong chords that gives us an image of a hero saving the day, thus earning the name "Eroica," or "heroic." I sat up in my seat with amazement as I saw his fingers pounce up and down on the piano, attacking it with his large hands. His hands moved so fast that they appeared as two blurs. The only thing that was clear was the music that poured through my ears and changed my feelings about the piano forever.

That day at the Wortham Theater also changed my life. Since then, I have found it a reward to practice the piano every day. Sometimes I am even scolded for playing too long, not doing my homework, and keeping everyone in my family up late at night. As a result of my hard training, I have received awards from several piano competitions, including two gold medals in the state competition of the University Interscholastic League (UIL). Both times a $500 scholarship to the University of Texas was part of the prize. Although the piano was never invented for competitions, winning has only made my love for the instrument increase and has inspired me to work even harder.

Also, I take private lessons at the Rice University Shepherd School of Music Preparatory Program. Once a week I meet with my teacher, Dariusz Pawlas, in the practice hall at the Shepherd School. I sit on the piano bench, and we talk about recent piano concerts or events that we have been to or heard about. He makes sure the conversation doesn't last longer than a couple of minutes because he is always eager to jump into the lesson. Dr. Pawlas loves music; it is revealed through his frantic pacing across the room and the passionate, whether slow or fast, movement of his hands as he conducts my playing. That is important to me because you cannot sell a product if you don't believe in it.

After we talk a bit, I play what I have worked on during the week and he critiques every passage. If Dr. Pawlas tells me to do something with my playing that I find very hard to do, he doesn't let me stop practicing it until I get it exactly as it should be played. He is gentle but firm, and it is this trait that leads to my success in music. The lessons are supposed to be an hour long, but Dr. Pawlas frequently keeps me at least thirty minutes beyond that, and he once kept me for three hours.

Playing the piano is not only important to me because of how it makes me feel, but because I use it to make a good name for Hispanics everywhere. I attend a high school that is predominantly white; and I often hear racial remarks about Hispanics. Students have asked me numerous times to mow their yards, and I have received other derogatory remarks. Oftentimes I am belittled by Caucasians my age and their parents because they think I am dumb, thuggish, or mischievous, just because I am Mexican American. I have stood up against many people when they have made racial comments, but sometimes not even this is enough. It is not until I play the piano for them and their parents that they realize that I am not dumb or from the ghetto. I use the piano to show people that Hispanics can be just as smart and talented as any person of any race.

As people figure this out for themselves, I will be at home sitting on a bench practicing my way into a career filled with music. I will let my fingers do all the communicating as I come closer with every turn of the page to a promising, exciting, and fulfilling grand finale.

waterloo street

perla melendez

I NEVER WANTED TO MOVE FROM THAT HOUSE over on Waterloo Street across from Alan and Eric, next door to Leslie and Brandon, who came over to play after breakfast every day till our Mamas called us in for the dinner that we were too hopped up on sweets to even eat, but we would play till then and sometimes after. Long games of Star Wars and dress-up, hopscotch with our feet too small to get across the great divide we had created for ourselves with the chalk that took up the whole of our little hands and fingers, always clasping onto what was there, right in front of us, right there. When we were dirty and didn't care, when hairy legs were alright to have, with scabby knees and dirty elbows won from leaning on the grass, on the dirt, in the flower beds, with knees grimy, hands sticky, hair oily and a bit musty from our little girl and boy sweat (too sweet to cringe at), there was nothing more exciting than the sound of the ice-cream truck, bells-a-ringing—it was like Christmastime every day of the week. No matter what the grown-ups said, no matter that he was a nose-picking, armpit-stained-shirt-wearing, dirty-money-in-his-mouth kinda guy who sold those *paletas*. They still tasted good in our six, seven, eight-year-old mouths, and I never wanted that reel of film to give way to anything new, anything else, because what we had was sacred and nothing is anymore with the house too small for guests and the walls too strange to paint because the landlord will definitely take note and get angry, maybe even write us a bill, fine us for wanting something of our own. If I had something of my own, I would definitely share it with whoever, whenever, but that day doesn't look like it's coming because it's been a long time coming that I, that we, have wanted something to call our own and make our home. Long time coming. Ever since we got kicked out by that hick who wanted to raise the rent even higher, maybe find a buyer who would destroy my swing set and cut down the tree that we planted on my seventh birthday after the rain knocked the other one down. He wanted someone to remodel the place, get rid of the clubhouse, and put up a fence so there wouldn't be any remnants of what we had so fun and free. I never wanted that cup of juice to spill and leave a stain on my purple dress now too short as I have grown up and outgrown things, but surely I have not outgrown that little dwelling that we called home on Waterloo Street.

childhood in English
Alicia Montero

BY LATE AFTERNOON, we were moving an old fridge we had
bought at the Dyer Street Swap-o-rama into the apartment when
the clouds suddenly gathered above us. My mother told my
brother and me to go inside as the rain crashed down on the
sloping street, my uncle's pickup truck, my grandfather's nose,
my coconut popsicle. I stood by the only window in the apartment, watching as they frantically covered up the beige dining
set and a couple of boxes left on the pickup truck with plastic
bags. I bit down into my popsicle, now melting a sugary white
liquid trailing down my wrists, tasting of something pleasant
and unfamiliar. That summer day of 1991 was the first time I
tasted El Paso rain.

◆

My parents had somehow come to hear about something
called the American Dream. It could have been on a pamphlet,
like in the old days, promising lands of vast fertility, unending
sunshine, and enduring crops, but only for the brave and daunt-
less to secure, only for those willing to work hard for it. Perhaps
my father had heard of it at work. He had been born in Ciudad
Juárez but had been working at a gas station in El Paso since he
was fifteen years old, trading a couple of sentences in English
for tips, washing and polishing cars to John Lennon's British
accent and Jimmy Hendrix's crying guitar, seducing American
women like he imagined Mick Jagger would. My mother was
uprooted from Parral, Chihuahua at the age of fifteen, having
fallen in love with my father, *feo, fuerte y formal.*

We moved from Ciudad Juárez to El Paso, fitting into boxes our clothes and shoes, framed photographs, LPs of Ricardo Montaner and the Beatles, leaving behind uniforms of Mexican private schools and my grandfather's rituals of sweeping his home inside and out, storytelling about his life as a *minero* in the afternoon, binge drinking on lazy Saturdays, and hosting repentant, somber meetings with *cristianos* who refused to watch television on Sundays. It had taken us more than two weeks to move in, and we had been unable to bring my mother's favorite *olla Presto* and white dishware given to my parents as a wedding present with the Hipermart price tag on the box. We were still eating twenty-five-cent hamburgers.

I could have asked them to rise from the ground, to come together in my hands, but instead they circled me, flying past my head, and I stood stunned, my tiny nails curling into my palms, watching the delicate motions of my homework assignments as they littered the monkey bars, the street, the unknown. I walked away, daydreaming that one day someone would find one of my papers and cherish it like an archeological artifact.

A basketball coach, holding one of my homework assignments that had escaped me, stopped me before I crossed the street. I looked back, hoping she had been impressed by my limited English vocabulary scribbled onto the now yellow and stained recycled paper.

"I have this for you and a piece of advice. You live in America now. Here, you don't write out all of your last names. See? Montero Cobos? Montero, that's all. Oh, and don't be throwing away your papers here. You do have a trash can at home, right?"

Mr. Hernandez pointed to the sign pinned to his shirt, and we knew he would not answer our question. "English only," it said. We struggled to ask him in English what we would get for reciting the time tables in the fastest time possible. I stepped to the front of the room. You can recite them in Spanish, if you'd like, he said, nobody will ever ask you, "Do you want cream with your coffee and what's nine times nine?" So, math in Spanish is fine.

Nueve por uno, nueve; nueve por dos, dieciocho; nueve por tres, veintisiete; nueve por cuatro, treinta y seis . . .

Finished in eight seconds. My team won that day. And every day Mr. Hernandez had us reciting time tables for caramel candy.

◆

It is not simple to remember my childhood days in English. But I do remember my nights. Watching shadows saunter past the apartment, laughter and breaking bottles disappearing into the night, the streetlight shining in and out onto my parents' bed—nights before school with classmates telling real funny stories about tripping their mothers, their little brothers falling from beds in the middle of the night, uncles smashing their thumbs with hammers, or Lupe or Tony dropping their lunch trays in the cafeteria. Before seeing canal rats make our $100-a-month apartment their home, finding roaches disappearing under our beds when turning on the lights to get ready for school in the morning, or hearing my mother complain about feeling rats crawling over her legs wrapped in bedsheets. Before longing to be an artist, flowers of Diego Velázquez, melting suns in the surrealist world of Joan Miró, suffering and pain of Picasso's "Weeping Woman," lost Van Gogh's ear and Matisse gold fish dancing on, inspired me. Before postcards from Toronto, New York, Cleveland, San Antonio, Los Angeles, New Orleans decorated my walls in a college dorm room. Before I lived the excitement of being home once again.

I was there, only a little girl, crying and sleepless.

"It's weak to cry in front of these *gringos*. Be strong. Never show them your pain, *m'ija*," my mother warned.

Watching shadows, tongue still tasting of rain. I am there again, no longer crying.

she-ra

juanita montoya

WHEN I WAS A LITTLE GIRL, my father used to call me She-Ra, after the heroine on the 80s cartoon "Masters of the Universe." I always thought of her as a strong, kick-butt, cone-bra-wearing chick. I had her pajamas, action figures, and even a lunch box with the matching thermos. I loved her. I really, really liked that nickname, and I admired what she stood for. My dad hasn't called me that in years. But every time I think about it, I smile inside and get that warmth that accompanies fond memories.

I have a T-shirt I found about a year ago with her picture on it. She's got a sword in her hand and is kicking the crap out of some alien guy. Maybe that's why I liked her so much. Even though she was a girl, even though she had blonde hair, she rocked. She wore gold go-go boots and saved the world at the same time, holding her own with the strong, shirtless males around her.

As I was buying the shirt, my mom asked me if my dad still called me She-Ra. That is when I realized that he hadn't. And I didn't know why, but it really hurt. I almost wanted to cry. I answered her with the one-worded thud of "No" and quickly paid the salesman as a way of changing the subject.

Maybe my dad thinks I don't need to hear that nickname anymore. Maybe he thinks I'm too old for a childhood cartoon. I don't know. But I know that I miss it.

My father and I have a healthy relationship. We simply don't have very much to talk about anymore. I hate that. I hate the fact that we don't have a favorite television show in common. I hate that he doesn't listen to rock n' roll anymore. I hate that the only thing that we really talk about is church. I hate that he doesn't like my red-colored hair, and what I really hate is that I'm no longer his little girl. I'm no longer his She-Ra.

But things are getting better. Slowly things are improving. If I'm honest with myself, I was partly to blame. I didn't care to see that while my father may not always care for the latest punk bands, he still knows more about Bob Dylan or Bruce Springsteen than anyone else I know. If he doesn't seem to pay attention to what I am reading, it may be because I don't offer to share. Our car rides home sometimes may be heavy with silence, but that's because I don't always speak up.

It doesn't always have to be this way. As I grow older, I will change, and so will he. And we'll notice what we have in common more than we'll notice our differences. To be close to my father, I don't have to be "Daddy's little girl." I can be myself and he can be who he is.

Things will be different.

MY TABOO

I STEADIED MY VOICE AS MUCH AS I COULD and hoped Cheryl wouldn't pick up on the falseness in it. "So, has he asked about me lately?"

There was an excruciating three-second pause. She's my best friend. Of course, she saw through my pitiful act.

"Uh, yeah. He said to tell you hi."

"Really?"

"He asks about you all the time, Juanita." I could hear her swallow. "Not details or anything, but he always wants to know how you're doing."

"Are you serious? And you never tell me?" My act was forgotten. "And why is he asking about me anyway? Why can't he call me and talk to me like a normal person if he's so concerned with what I'm doing!"

I was furious. And she knew it.

◆

I knew Ryan for eighteen months. I remember the first time I saw him. It was on the first day of a new job. I was sitting in the break room eating a pack of Skittles and drinking a can of Coke, and he strolled into the room. I was immediately drawn to him, to his worldly look and his confident stature. I bent my nose back into Dreiser's *Sister Carrie*. I could feel his steady gaze as he sat down directly across from me and ate a bagel. He ate perfectly too, I remember thinking. I couldn't focus on the page in front of me and kept reading the same sentence over and over and over. I have never been able to finish that book since.

For the first month or so, we simply chatted a little when we ran into each other. But I began to hear rumors around the office that he was asking about me. I decided to see for myself and went to visit him in his office. I was so impressed. Twenty years old and he had his own office. We admitted our attraction to each other. I loved his hazel eyes and he loved the golden-brown hue of my skin. Such a contrast to his pale color. We exchanged numbers and talked the next day for two hours.

At first, it was exciting. We took our lunch breaks together, talked for even more hours on the phone. But he slowly began to break promises. He'd ask me to go out with him, but he wouldn't show up. He'd promise to call me, and he wouldn't. When I would confront him about it, he would come up with some ridiculous, but completely believable, excuses. When we would take our breaks outside, he would pull cigarettes from his gold carton of Marlboros he kept in his chest pocket. He knew I hated smoking.

We had a strange relationship. The only physical contact we ever had were a couple of hugs. But what we lacked in the physical part of the relationship, I felt we made up in other ways. We understood each other. I guess you could say he was my Renaissance Man. He spoke three languages and had lived all over the world. He would entertain me with stories about the time he played hockey in Beijing or when he lived in a tiny South American village. He's well read and writes. We are both dreamers, magic bean buyers, the kind of people who live life with music playing in our heads. That is why we got along so well.

The last time I talked to him I saw him in his office about a month after I quit working in the building. He tilted his head just a little to the side, widened his eyes, and smiled that special smile that was reserved just for me. He apologized for treating me badly. I forgave him immediately and told him basically not to think twice about it. Ah, but I did. I thought about it all day long, so I called him and told him that he had treated me horribly. He made me feel ugly. Desperate. Weak. Things I never wanted to be. I haven't talked to him since.

Ryan is my taboo because he is my weakness. When I find out he's asking about me or when I think about him too much, all my feelings resurface. I have to pretend he never existed. He let me know I can be naïve and pathetic. He reminded me of what it feels like to have someone make me feel insecure. I'm not upset with him anymore because of the way he treated me, but at myself because I allowed it. I have never let myself emotionally connect with anyone the way I did with him. He was able to smash the walls I had built. He hopped over my barbed wire fences, and I despise him for it. I gave him too much power. Ryan is the secret I try to keep from myself.

◆

As quickly as my anger rises, it drains away as quickly, leaving me empty and spent. I ask Cheryl, "Cheryl, do you think I should call him?"

"No, Juanita! He's a nice guy and all, but he's not boyfriend material. You can do better."

I stop listening at this point. I have her speech memorized.

grandmother's stories

Melissa A. Moran

THIS IS THE STORY I WANT TO TELL. It's a story about the women in my family and the life lessons they have shared with me. It's about their struggles and the influences that have made me who I am today.

◆

It was a hot summer night in a border town near the Rio Grande Valley. My mother was twenty-two years old and lay in bed waiting for sleep. It was a restless night for her. She was eight months pregnant with me, and my sister Monica was in bed next to her. Monica was only a year and a half and lay quietly in sleep. But it was too hot for my mother to find any comfort.

That night she had decided to spend the weekend with her mother. It was something she had done since her father had passed away a year before. But this night was different from any other night. While she lay in bed, she heard a cry that made her sit up with a stunned heart. A piercing wail cut through the night's air. Only one thing could cry like that. My mother felt a cool breeze and sat up paralyzed in fear. She hoped, perhaps, it was the neighbors. But no, she had to be sure. She rushed out of bed as fast as she could and made her way to my grandmother's room. She didn't bother to turn on the lights. Her eyes were adjusted to the dark and she knew her way well around the house.

"*¡Amá, levántate! ¡Creo que oí a La Llorona!*" She gently shook my grandmother so she could wake her and confirm what she had just heard. It may seem unusual to be awakened in the middle of the night because of something like this, but not for my superstitious grandmother. They both sat in dark silence, waiting for the sound that my mother had heard. My mother could hear the pounding of her heart in her ears as she tried to calm herself. So many thoughts raced through her mind. Were they safe in the house? Where was her husband when she needed him, and what could he be doing? That afternoon when my father had returned home from work, he decided he wanted to go out for the night. "Where are you going?" she had asked him.

"I'm going out," my father answered.

"But where are you going? Why can't you stay home? Why do you always have to go out?"

My father would always answer the same way. "I'm going out." He'd quickly shower and change. My mother stood powerless as she watched him go.

"*Vas a ver*," my mother would scream. "One day I'll leave you!" But it was an empty threat. She knew it and so did he. How could she make it on her own with two children?

My grandmother and mother did not have a long wait for the next cry to come again. It was carried in a strong wind that lifted the curtains as the air circulated its way around the room. "*Sí, es la Llorona*," my grandmother confirmed. She was certain it was her since she had heard her once before. My mother took a deep breath and hurried back to her room to make sure my sister had slept through the horrifying ordeal.

◆

"*Amá, ¿pero cómo sabes que era La Llorona?*" I asked my grandmother again and again when I was a little girl. How did she know it was the Llorona crying that night?

"*La Llorona*," my grandmother would tell me, "was the spirit of a woman who was cursed to walk the earth because of the terrible sin she had committed."

"But what sin, Grandma?" Even though I had heard her stories before, they never stopped captivating me.

"Because," my grandmother would tell me in Spanish, "she was a poor woman. She didn't even have enough money to feed her children. Then her husband left her, and some say she had a lover who didn't want a woman who had children. No one knows exactly. But they do know this. She drowned her children and killed herself. Then she went to heaven and God told her that her soul will never rest until she paid for what she did. *¡Ahora duérmete, huerca!*"

But how could I sleep after hearing my grandmother's stories? I had so many questions yet to ask. Why had her husband left her? How could she even think about killing her own children? Didn't she love them?

I lay in my soft bed snuggled close to my grandmother. I often fell asleep smelling the sweet smell of her Oil of Olay and waiting to hear *La Llorona*. I didn't worry that I might be scared; nothing seemed scary when I was sleeping next to my grandmother.

In my young mind I saw *La Llorona* as a mother and I felt sadness for her. Perhaps *La Llorona*'s soul wasn't wandering the earth cursed by God like my grandmother believed, but because she regretted the choice she made.

I never did hear the cries of *La Llorona*. Now that I think back to the stories my grandmother told me, I realize that they have helped me become the person I am today. I feel I am stronger than other women in my family. But maybe one day if I am feeling powerless, I will hear *La Llorona* and it will remind me that all is not lost.

Taboo

MY WEEKENDS and occasionally some weeknights are filled with my colorful misadventures out with the girls. They usually involve me sitting up front in Maggie's pearly white Lexus RX300, cruising downtown close to midnight with the windows and sunroof open, radio blaring to whatever the latest song happens to be. The warm Houston air is filled with excitement.

Groups of guys walking the crowded city streets holler out to us when we pass by. Groups of guys looking to score line the streets in their little sports cars or big SUVs. They pass us by and check us out. Sometimes they smile at us and sometimes they call out wanting to know our names and where we are going. Whatever it is they say or do, we usually have something witty to say back and then giggle hysterically. It's exciting living in the moment; I feel adventurous, yet protected being inside the car.

But while I'm out having fun and living my life, I can't help feeling that I'm hanging on to my friends by their skirt tails, flying high on adrenaline, and running as fast as I can just to keep up in my gem-studded, blue denim Bandolino shoes. And it's not easy running in three-inch heels, especially if you have twenty-something years of inhibitions pulling you back. Now that I'm older, I find myself having to make decisions on issues that I never thought of while I was growing up. Issues like will I be able to have casual sex with a guy without getting emotionally involved with him?

When I was younger, the idea of having a "friend with benefits" never crossed my mind. Coming from a Mexican-American family, it simply wasn't done. At least, that's what was preached and drilled into my head. Good girls don't do those things unless you're married and even then it wasn't talked about. But I'm no longer a teenager sneaking in late from one of my high school dates and having to answer to my father. I'm my own person now, living my own life, and I have to make my own decisions and be able to live with them. My friend Maria playfully gives me a soft shove and says things like, "Girl, just go get you some." I can't help rolling my eyes in her direction. Easier said than done.

◆

Maria once came up with a plan I like to call Operation Hook Up. The plan was to meet up with her friend one night, someone I had a slight crush on, and get us alone. We met at this trendy bar in Uptown, and Maria left early so I could ride home with her friend. The night went exactly as planned. We left the bar together, and I jumped into his truck with such confidence. I felt daring and determined. As we started to talk he asked me what type of guys I was interested in. In my moment of bravado, I answered him by saying, "Well, what if I said you were my type?"

He hesitated for only a second. "What exactly is it that you're looking for? I mean, I want to have sex with you but anything more than that I'm not ready for."

I struggled for a second while the reality of the situation set in. I was no longer the one in control; the plan had been changed. What Maria and I had not thought of was that this plan involved another human being who had motives and ideas of his own. I had to think of something to say, but how could I respond to something like that?

"I'm not looking for anything serious right now either," I said. "I'm busy with school and right now that's my first priority." That was the truth, I thought to myself. But was I seriously ready to have casual sex with someone I know I'd run into every once in a while?

Then he grabbed my hand and held it while he drove the truck with the other. His touch startled me as much as his response had. It struck me as sexy because it felt natural. It was intimate. He continued to talk about other things I really can't remember. I kept hearing his words over and over in my mind. All the while he was still holding my hand. It occurred to me maybe that's what I wanted, real intimacy.

I had thought I was ready to handle the situation physically and emotionally, but I was mistaken. Then, for reasons that I still can't understand, I became angry with his answer. But why should I be angry? Wasn't that exactly what I had planned all along? I felt anger toward him for complicating the situation but even more so with myself. I was the stupid one for thinking I could go through with this.

I should have jumped right out of his truck when we reached my house but I stayed. Part of me was still committed to do what I had set out to do. The other part of me wanted to go back to my adolescent years and run home to daddy. But I kissed that guy instead. I couldn't understand it at the time and I really don't understand it now. Looking back I shouldn't have stayed in the truck because no good came out of it. He kept wanting to go further and further. But it was my decision to make, and in the end, I couldn't bring myself to do it. I haven't spoken to the guy since. How could I face him? What would I say?

I came out of the situation with a better sense of who I am. But how will I handle myself next time? Will it leave me more confused on what kind of woman I want to become? Am I ready to take on this type of relationship? Even though my friends tease me about my reluctance, I still can't help thinking that for me it would be a life-altering experience. One I'm not yet ready to handle.

Down Quisqueya Heights
Génesis Piña

ANY OTHER DAY, I don't mind walking down the block. But today, I am walking by myself. As soon as I step out of my building at 190th Street and Broadway, I can tell that summer is definitely here. Music is being played loudly from all different places, but it is Juan Luis Guerra's song, *Visa para un sueño,* that I can make out clearly. The men, both *trabajadores* and *borrachos*, are sitting outside, playing dominoes and drinking beer. There is Rafael with his big beer belly, laughing as the men engage in some sexual joke. The women are sitting outside their buildings, gossiping as the younger children ride their bikes up and down the block.

As usual, Quisqueya Heights is full of the common Dominican language and people. And it seems as if today will be like any other day, but today, it will be different.

Today, my girlfriends are not with me, and that means that the guys, the *tigres*, as my mother calls them, will have their eyes set on me. They will be at their usual corner on their block, talking, rolling a joint, or handling some drug deal. The *tigres* will be busy doing something, and as soon as they see you coming, they will be ready for you. They start to talk and try to get with you, not necessarily to get you to be their *novia*, but simply to prove to everyone else that they have "Game." That they can get a conversation going, get you smiling, and eventually, get your number. If they can't, then usually they'll just insult you. You really can't escape it.

Usually, I don't mind what they say, as long as I'm with my girlfriends. When I'm with my girlfriends, the guys can tell me that I am pretty and they can tell me that I'm ugly too, because I won't let that bother me. My girlfriends understand because they go through it too. Together, we can handle it; but today, I am by myself. I have to make sure to walk quickly past the guys, but not too fast because I don't want to trip like Lucero. *Pobre* Lucero.

Lucero is this one girl from around my way. She is one of the lighter-skinned Latinas from our neighborhood, with straight blonde hair and pretty green eyes. And unlike many of us, she doesn't wear the little dresses, the halter tops or the short skirts in the summer. No, Lucero is not like us. You won't find her wearing gold hoop earrings or a gold necklace with her name on it. Instead, Lucero wears the polo shirts and the khaki pants, like the ones she wears today. Oh Lucero . . . she doesn't even wear the right clothes or the right things. It's because of this that the *tigres* call her a "Gringa Wannabe."

I remember seeing Lucero from my window one day, as she came out of the bodega with a bag of oranges. And I also remember how her long khaki corduroy pants made her trip and fall. It happened so quickly. One minute, Lucero was walking and the next minute she was on the floor.

One by one, her oranges rolled out onto the street, and one by one, the guys began to laugh at her and shout in English with their Dominican accent: "Ghet the orange! Ghet the orange!" They did not help her get up and they did not help her get the oranges. All I saw was Lucero trying to get all six of them, but she couldn't. Two of her oranges had already gotten run over by a car and one had rolled down the curb, to some place where she could not see it. I don't know what happened to the other orange, but I remember everything else.

Lucero was standing on the corner, holding her two *naranjas*, one in each hand with the bag under her right arm. As she stood on that corner, she waited for that red light to rescue her from the embarrassment she must have been feeling. I know she

génesis piña

cried, because as soon as she crossed the street, she began to dry her eyes with her white polo shirt.

I don't know exactly why she cried, but I'm pretty sure that she must have cried out of the embarrassment she had to endure on that day. She must have cursed those khaki corduroy pants over and over again for making her fall on that specific day, when all the guys were there. She must have wondered if they would have helped her if she were not a "Gringa Wannabe." I'm pretty sure, because since that day Lucero has not gone back to that bodega or to the block. The only thing I am sure of is that I don't want what happened to her to happen to me. That's why I am careful about how I walk, praying that I don't become a Lucero.

I am very careful when I'm walking down the block because I know that the guys already see me coming. And besides worrying about not landing on the ground, I'm worrying about the way I look. I have to make sure that I look the way they expect me to look. I've made sure that my top is fitted and that my pants are tight enough to show them my curves. My hair is up in a big bun with enough gel in it, and I'm wearing my big gold earrings. I've made sure that when the guys talk to me, they will see that I am one of them.

I know that they see me the minute that I step onto the edge of the rugged sidewalk, waiting for traffic to subside, before going on to their block. I know that they've seen me because I see them moving around. They're trying to find the best way to approach me and I already know what to expect—it's the usual, "Psst . . . Psst . . . *Oye!*"—as if that's my name! But at the moment, I don't know where it's coming from, because they're all looking at me. It may have come from the guys playing dominoes or from the guys near the arcade machine, but I'm not sure. All I know is that I pretend not to hear them, and that doesn't even help.

Eventually, as I am walking, a pair of white Nike sneakers blocks my path. I don't bother to look up at who they belong to, but I can hear the voice and the line he uses on me. *"Oye, mami, you looking real nice. Can you give me a minute?"* I try not to pay him any attention, but he keeps at it. "But damn, you can't even give me a minute?" He keeps going on, asking me for my digits, and I keep on ignoring him and walk away. But it's not over yet.

On the next block, I already see Raul flashing his *billetes*, pretending to go and buy something at the bodega, when all he really wants is for me to see that he has money. I see Juancito shyly looking at me and Tito parked right in front of the guys, looking at me as he stands by his brand-new car. I see them all waiting to show off and prove who's got game. In the meantime, I'm walking real fast, trying to get off that block without any one of them coming up to me. I fidget with my purse and pretend that I am looking for something. I pretend to be busy so no one will talk to me, but Chelo doesn't care. He comes up to me and walks by my side. He tries to make me stop, so I can talk to him. He reaches for my arm, then my hand, and tries to make eye contact. I give him a fake smile, it's the one that says *hi there, go away now*. But Chelo doesn't get the hint, and as I try to pull away, I look up at his face.

I always try to look at their faces because if there's a cute face, then maybe one of them will get my real digits instead of the fake ones that I usually give out. But that doesn't happen now. Chelo isn't cute, so he doesn't get my digits but he keeps trying and keeps on walking with me, that is—until the end of the block. The block ends here, so he stops. As if going to the next block will be intruding on the guys from that block or something like that.

It doesn't matter though that Chelo has stopped, because on the next block there will be another guy just like him, another one trying to prove that he's got game. Walking down the Quisqueya blocks is like meeting someone new every time my feet move a pace. I'll meet a Julio or a Manuel or some guy that might say I'm pretty or not. Usually, I'm ready for anything that the guys have to say to me, but today it's very likely that I won't say anything back. Today, I know that I am by myself and that there will be more of them than there will be of me.

Listening for Your Name
Remy Ramirez

THE KEY TO PARTNER DANCING, as I understand it, is giving up. *Rag doll rag doll* you are thinking, but that's not it either. Make not a mess of yourself, but rather, push back on the palm just enough to be sent directly. Remove all thoughts; no counting at all, and no telling yourself to remove all thoughts because that is the death: nervous is worse. From nervous comes counting, counting breeds prediction. And it is the exact moment that you consider your future with this man that the people shake their heads sadly at the ground; that dark stubbing, your nose in his armpit.

(But don't stop putting flowers on your table, in your windows, behind your ears. Don't stop buying lingerie to wear for your cat. Don't stop listening for your name. Don't stop drinking coffee on the weekends or taking your vitamins or meditating on the powers of antiaging antioxidants antibiotics. Don't stop checking your cell for messages. For Proactiv is not just an infomercial, it is 2.5 heavenly percentages of benzoyl peroxide; we are each a living decision.)

In 2003 I was studying on exchange in Granada, Spain, and I traveled by bus to three of the "Pueblos Blancos," white cities in Andalucia, in warm weather in a light sweater. With mostly older Spaniards, we circled fields of tall grass for hours—green and undisturbed, but not haunted, the way so much of nature is to me. We turned a corner and abruptly the hills were skinned to a bright knobby bone of houses, steeples, *carnicerías*.

And they apologized to us as we gathered outside in the blank stare of the white city. It was Sunday; the shops were closed, and we could not buy their handmade leather purses or their ugly pink belts. Be back at the bus by one.

I took pictures of average things: orange blossom trees, the square, yellow clock tower cobblestone home baby black insides of white houses in the white city, a little girl with ragged black hair, stroking a wall between potted red flowers.

I was walking up the little breaking roads, winding into the pueblo's narrow, thinly aired sky. A woman stood outside the door of a white church, looking solicitous but bored. I remember nothing about her, except that she didn't advertise and she wasn't rude and, once inside, she would tell me nothing.

Of Jesus in a box. A glass box. A glass coffin box, his eyes closed, and his long body oily looking and wrong looking. White, for one thing, because Spaniards are white, or because clouds or pages of books or nail clippings are white. And ill-painted. His cheeks were rosy with the excitement of his final resting place, here on a small hill, guarded by a listless Catholic woman zombie-ing about the Sunday chores. And roses in his hair, hurting him. And of course, his wonderful red blood, still and dried to his face and feet and fingers. Someone had come to leave flowers.

I began joking in my head. *This is hysterical!* I took pictures that would come out badly from the glare of the flash on the shiny glass walls of his box. *This is so wrong that it's great.* Snow White in her awful glass casing, full of apple and white skin and red lips, unfinished business left in the kingdom, dwarves mourning. Had she been a Christian?

Boxed up Jesus, pretty with his hands crossed over his slim belly and his calves flexed from fighting Satan, his toes chipping off at the cuticle, the way corpses do.

I stared at his empty, dead face. What should I have said to Jesus at his grave? *You were so lonely when you left us; one thing leads to another: fire, stone bridges, glue, the Titanic sank at night and people drowned in that black water; first they were*

---

afraid, then they became very cold, then all the noises were a painful blabber and their lungs were full of that black water and then they were gone forever. You took their little cup and turned it over.

But I'm not mad. Come back with a belly full of air and make a label of all decisions like Kahlil Gibran: "Master, tell us of roses in vases, in windows, in our hair. Speak of control and fear. Explain this satin nightie I wear night after night with a pillow between my legs and a cat in the corner, and the coffee on automatic timer and the hating the aging and mirror." You put wings to my face so that I might be free, but drugs are what we're made of. Tiny pink hearts full of an obdurate envy and Retin-A. Science cramps to loosen us from the weight of your memory, to make us sing like comets exploding in the air, like lights dying into a sky where no one lives. But we never stood a chance. They buried your sadness into the ground. They grew vegetables in your grief. We eat to gut ourselves into little shells, and sit back down in the ground with you.

And like kindergarteners we pile our toys to stay busy till someone— you, not you, anyone— says our names.

Or is the secret in giving up? Remove all thoughts; no counting at all because that is the death: nervous is worse. Rag doll rag doll flopping her knees buckling her dress crumpling. Or is that not it either? You push back just enough to be sent directly to your little glass box in forever. Or just don't even consider the future.

Remove all thoughts; no counting at all because that is the death.

The woman's heels echoed curtly as she arranged pamphlets on a fold-up table in the back of the chapel. Outside, the Spaniards were feeding their flowers and their children, and things were darkening just a little. I pushed a euro into the donation box, which landed with a thud against the empty, wooden inside.

Leaving to Missouri
Evelin Rivera

"ARE YOU READY TO GO?" I remembered Sergeant Perkins asking a few minutes past three in the afternoon on the thirteenth of March.

It had finally hit me; I realized that I was leaving for basic training up in Missouri within hours. I was to leave everything back home, the smell of chile rellenos, my soft, white feather pillow, as well as the smiles and the warm hugs from my father, my siblings, and that one hug from my stepmother. The next few hours were as dark as a night without any moonlight. While waiting for my recruiter, no one said anything; it seemed as if everyone had finally realized that it was real. I was leaving home.

When the green Geo Prism drove by and my recruiter parked in my driveway, tears began filling my dad's brown eyes. He held me tighter as if his hugs would make basic training disappear. As the sergeant with her straight shoulders and head held high in pride wearing her pickle-colored uniform knocked on my front door, my throat began to knot. My words couldn't come out. I wanted to tell my family how much I loved them and how much I would miss them, but I knew it would only make things worse. I remember my recruiter broke our funereal silence when she said, "Well, sir, it is time to take your daughter to the hotel where she will stay tonight and then be shipped to Missouri early in the morning tomorrow."

It had been three months since I had taken my oath as a U.S Army soldier, and the paperwork was finally completed. The many visits by my recruiter, Sergeant Perkins, had finally ceased. No more phone calls repeating her sweet words stating, "the Army is the best choice you will ever make. I can assure you that you will never regret it." I found it hard not to believe her when soldiers posed proud with their heads up high on the posters and they said only wonderful things about the military in the basic training video. I knew that joining the service would be one of the major and most critical decisions I would ever make in my life. Everything was ready to go; my paperwork stating that I was almost blind, my blood type O positive, and my height at 61 inches was all signed and stamped by higher personnel. Everything was now well organized in my black Army-labeled portfolio.

I was going to prove to myself and my family that I could do it on my own. I wasn't that little girl who couldn't defend herself anymore. Even if I didn't know how yet, I was sure that the military would teach me how to defend myself. It was obvious to me that the new soldier wasn't the only one in the family who felt a cold, empty stomach that couldn't be filled up with food or water. My dad's dark brown eyes didn't have the shine that I was used to seeing during the last seven years since he and I had been reunited in the United States after he had left El Salvador. In a way, I guess he felt as if he would lose me again, just like he had done when I was a baby and he had come to the United States trying to find a better life for me. The newly formed wrinkles on his forehead seemed never-ending. As my stepmom helped me pack, I finally started to understand the seriousness of my decision. I remember her giving me one hug—a hug that I had never felt before. Her beating heart and her warmth made me feel as if everything was going to be okay. My little brother, too young to understand, would only innocently say, *"Papi, mañana vamos a traer a Evelin con el carro . . . "* In his mind, I was going to leave the house for a day and the next day after school he would have me right back. My sister in her shy way only smiled at me, not really understanding why I was leaving them but knowing that soon I would return home.

By noon I was in need of some acrylic nails, having bitten every single nail on my fingers down to the nub, and now I found myself biting my lip anxiously waiting for Sergeant Perkins to call me and let me know she was on her way. By two o'clock I had received phone calls from everyone, including friends from elementary and middle school years; even the priest and his family had called to wish me luck. Time that day flew right past me; I spent it mainly trying to hug my family as much as possible. This would be my first trip ever . . . I hadn't been allowed to go to camp when I was young. "Snakes will bite you!" I remember my parents warning me. This would be my test as well as my dad's. He would finally have to give his little girl up, watch her grow and mature in basic training.

As I picked up my blue and gold Nautica bag, I knew that this was the moment I had been waiting for—the day I could survive on my own. I remember that last hug that my father gave me. He wrapped me in his arms and slowly laid his head on my shoulder while his brown eyes filled with tears. He kissed my forehead and said, "God will always be with you. Don't ever forget that." Closing the door of my house was the hardest thing I will ever do, knowing that on one side of the door my parents would start crying and on the other my tears would finally become victims of gravity. As I sat in the passenger side, I looked up in the sky and could only wonder, why did I join? Is this what I really want? Will I be able to do it on my own?

That day I thought freedom would be leaving my parents, not ever realizing that my drill sergeants would make me see things clearly once in Missouri. Now that I look back, I realize this was the day I learned that being independent has a very heavy price. The price of leaving great moments with your family locked in a vault until you return. I also realized that my dad would finally understand that his little girl had now turned into an independent woman able to pay her rent and her car note. This independent woman would be capable of making wise decisions like getting and maintaining a good job and staying in school. The independent woman who no longer needed daddy to pay rent or wake her up to go to work.

my cousin and me

THE LARGE SIGN in front of the main office stating "THE NEW AND RENEWED RENWICK MANOR APARTMENTS" sold the exterior of the apartments, while the inside was falling to pieces. Cracks on the walls and a cream-colored carpet now turned a dark brown. The need for shampooing or a new carpet never captured the main office's attention. The neighborhood women gossiped across the opened windows, letting cool air into their apartments.

It was the summer of 1990. I found myself spending valuable time with my aunt and her first baby, rattling his toys and making choo-choo sounds with his train. I was nine years old, my short golden-brown hair already insisting on turning a darker color. Aunt's newborn, now six months old, had turned into my favorite entertainment. He lived next to our green and white apartments that had been painted on the outside a hundred times.

On this day, just like every other day, I confronted the curb that stood in the middle of the street that divided my house from my cousin's house. It stood in the middle teasing me, knowing that once I would try to put my foot on it, I would fall and land on my bottom. It had been a test for several months. Every weekend I would try to defeat it, yet I always found myself failing. Being a short four feet ten inches at the age of nine made the curb of almost two feet tall seem like an impossible obstacle whether with my cousin in my arms or alone.

My baby cousin loved to be carried and to feel my warmth since I spent most of my time at his house. He was like a teddy bear to me, calling me to hug him, squeeze his cheeks, and tickle his stomach. His light-brown eyes gleamed like a ray of sun, and his hands reaching out to you would make even the strongest rock come tumbling down. He still had that newborn fragrance that makes your nose want to stay attached to his neck or his little arm trying to seize as much of it as possible.

One day after playing with my cousin for a couple of minutes, I made up my mind to carry him across the street, over the curb, and up the stairs to my house. I picked him up, like a soldier picks up his weapon ready for combat—not with the same grip but rather with determination for success and triumph. This wasn't my first time trying to carry him across the street, but this time I was determined to prevail. I loved carrying my cousin and he loved for me to do so, but as he was almost half of my size, it could be difficult. His tiny toes now passed my belly button making it hard to get a grip on his diaper bottom. I looked like an elderly woman trying to pick up a sack of potatoes; the weight was too heavy for my capability.

I began the journey across the busy parking lot that we were taught not to cross by the parents who kept most of the children playing indoors due to the *borrachos* who drove carelessly after a big night of celebration with alcohol. I still remember feeling the gravel underneath my black tennis shoes causing a greater tension on my feet due to the added weight. Then, when I finally had reached my destination, I held my cousin's bottom with a tighter grip and looked at him while he smiled at the sky in search of the singing birds. I lifted my right foot to the height of the yellow curb. Then, as I progressed to lead my other foot off the ground, I suddenly found myself looking straight up in the sky. I held my cousin even tighter as I felt my body hit the ground with my cousin on top of my stomach, which thankfully served as a pillow for his landing. As the dust lifted itself to cover our clothing, I heard the scream of pain and anguish coming from my baby cousin. The pale look in my face and the shaking of my hands made me guilty of the crime of making my cousin cry. I nervously tried to calm him down and also made sure he wasn't hurt and that there was no sign of bruises or blood. I tried to hug him tighter or make him laugh, but it was too late. My grandmother came running out of the house with a frightened look on her face, proclaiming, *"¡un día de estos lo vas a matar!"* She snatched my cousin from my tiny arms, repeating the phrase over and over. Her comment only made me wonder why I would want to kill my cousin. I loved him and I just wanted to bring him over to my house to have someone to play with. Why did she assume I was trying to kill him when I only wanted to play with him? One way or another, I would always get in trouble with my grandmother. Not many things have changed; I still manage to make her angry. Every time I made my cousin cry she was quick to remind me that I could end up killing him or sending him to an emergency room. As my punishment was being determined, my aunt defended me, "She's only a child, mom. Accidents happen . . . and he's not even hurt. He landed on top of her." She would talk to my grandmother until she would give in and forgive me for my sin.

I knew that I had gotten in trouble enough for the day, but tomorrow I would insist on trying to cross the parking lot and get over the curb successfully, holding him tight to my stomach. Now that I look back, I realize that I could have easily gotten either one of us hurt, especially with him being so fragile and small. I also realize that that's one of the reasons my cousin and I are still really close even today. We enjoy the same music, attend concerts, and often I help him with his homework. Now I even advise him on girl problems.

My grandmother always thought of my punishment, but to this day I don't remember that she ever punished me for falling. In a way, I guess she knew it was an accident. Her tenderness and caring ways made her give in to anything her *primera nieta* requested from her. My aunt always defended me and never accused me of wrongdoing, even though I'm sure she knew that her son could easily get hurt. Her charming smile widens every time she tells grandma, *"Ay, Mami, no se enoje . . . ¡están jugando!"* Even today she defends me against any comments or any accusations. I believe that she's so caring with me because my mother wasn't there to defend me, so she felt the need to protect me against harm or wrongdoing.

Challenges have always been a major part of my life and to insist on overcoming challenges has always been my reward. My determination leads me to success. It's very funny how a couple of inches of cement would make us trip and fall then and how today it seems so normal to step over the curb. What seemed an impossible challenge then is only a matter of taking a larger step now.

My Yellow Treasure

THE UNKNOWN GENTLEMAN with his slender figure and sweet smile reminded me of my grandpa Moncho. This was the second time my family in the United States had asked him to help. This time my grandma, my cousin, and I were protected in his home in Matamoros, Mexico. He was taking a chance in having three female immigrants in his house as he had done before for other members of my family.

He had never seen me but he already had my gift folded neatly in a brown box in his dark wooden drawer. The outside of the package was dull and simple. As I opened the box, the bright yellow color of the dress made even the plain box look as if it was covered with life. I held my golden treasure within the dark brown box tight with both arms. It was a sleeveless dress with two white stripes hanging from my shoulders to my belly; the rest was golden. It crawled to my knees showing off my small shoulders. I had never seen anything like it. Back in El Salvador, life was a struggle, and in order for me to have a new dress, my parents had to work extra in other *milpas* or buy less *frijoles* and *arroz* for the weekly groceries.

To my knowledge I've never looked good in yellow; my light yellowish skin tone looks pale when a gold or a light color covers it. However, everyone (my grandmother, my cousin, and the sweet gentleman) promised that it looked wonderful; it made me look like a princess. My grandma, who had risked her life crossing the border again with a seventeen year old and an eight year old, still remembers how my now-lost golden hair matched the dress. The day that I wore the dress for the first time the nameless gentleman risked his life and reputation by taking me to the carnival. I remember the giant white circle that amazed me every time it circled round and round against the sky. He told my grandma and I how he wanted me to remember Mexico as a wonderful experience, with a lively atmosphere and great people. He said that we had gone through too much, that now we needed to be pampered as much as possible. I guess he was just nice to everyone because throughout his life he never had children or a wife to share his time with. He had so much energy and no grandchildren to play around him.

I remember this sweet gentleman, who was barely able to pick up my eight-year-old body to give me a hug and a kiss on my forehead. It still amazes me how nice he was to me. Every day after his long, exhausting day working in the *milpa* under the hot, bright sun, he stopped in little shops and bought me *mango con chile*. The taste of the mango engulfed in hot sauce in a clear plastic bag called my taste buds with its intoxicating taste.

We had only spent a short week at his house when a stranger named Jaime called the sweet gentleman on the telephone. I wasn't able to put together the pieces to the puzzle, but somehow the person on the phone was excited to finally hear me. This stranger who called would turn out to be my father. Now, after eight years, the twenty-six-year-old young man would finally embrace his daughter after leaving El Salvador in search of a better life across the border for his parents as well as for his newborn daughter.

The night before I left the sweet, unknown gentleman's house I made sure that the piece of gold he had given me would stay with me. Early the next morning as the rooster began to sing his morning melody, there was chocolate and *pan dulce* ready for us to eat. The walls of his house were made of clay, and most of the lighting came from the *candil* that was fired by a small amount of gas in a container that soaked a piece of cloth pointing to the top. The *candil* produced a longer than normal shadow on the wall, making him look over six feet tall. At his house I began to understand that not even a five-star hotel would ever make me feel as comfortable and warm as this house had done.

It was a beautiful day in October when my grandmother, my cousin, and I finally reached our destination in Houston, Texas. When I arrived at a two-bedroom apartment clustered with boxes and beds that barely left a walkway to the living room and the bathroom, I was introduced to my father. After the hugs and the story of how I had come along, I felt comfortable and began unpacking my little bag. I bragged about my new dress and they insisted that I try it on. I hurried to the room and slid the golden dress over my head, the iridescent skirt swirling down to my knees. As I walked out of the room, my golden curls bounced above the clustered boxes. My uncles and father sat around and smiled while I twirled around with my hands on my waist. Again I was told that I looked like a princess. My newfound family enjoyed every second that I modeled my yellow dress to them.

The day that my yellow dress had to leave me because of the lack of space and the fact that there were plenty of new dresses to replace it, I wanted to fold it and keep it next to my precious teddy bears. That day, at the age of eleven, I finally realized that I couldn't force my wider shoulders into it anymore.

Now, after approximately sixteen years, I sit with my grandma Carmen and smile when we remember the nameless gentleman. Her smile widens every time she starts her story and ends with a *"¿te acuerdas cuando?"* and my doubtful face answers for me. I really don't remember most of the story; I do know that I loved the yellow dress. The warmth that it brought just by laying still on my bed getting ready to slide on my body or by hanging with the rest of the dresses in my closet. I remember getting a single letter from the sweet, unknown gentleman and then never hearing from him again. The last memory of him I still carry with me is that morning when I walked out of his modest house, his slender figure standing at the door waving good-bye to us.

Becoming Latina
E. M. Rodriguez

I was unpacking my suitcase when she said it.

It was my senior year in high school, and I was dutifully making the rounds of the colleges where I'd been accepted, trying to narrow down my choices. I was at one of those special weekends for prospective students and was settling into my hostess's room.

I had my back to her when she spoke. "You're pretty light, aren't you?"

I held my breath for a moment, feeling my chest tighten, and smoothed out the sleeve of the shirt I was holding. Her tone had been friendly, but the words struck a nerve. This weekend was supposed to be for "women of color," and I wasn't at all sure I belonged here.

With blue eyes and pale skin, I was well aware that I didn't "look" Latina and felt like an impostor for being there. I'd almost decided not to come at all because I was afraid I wasn't "Latina enough" and was sure the other girls would wonder what the *gringa* was doing there.

"My father is from Peru, but my mother's family is Swedish," I said quietly.

"Oh," she replied and smiled, switching the subject to all the activities available on campus.

◆

I think the weighty question of whether or not I was Latina first came up in elementary school, probably when I was in second grade. Filling out standardized test forms, I was stumped as to whether I should check off "Hispanic" or "White (non-Hispanic)".

I raised my hand to ask for help from one of the teacher's aides. A harried woman more concerned with students who didn't know their addresses or how to spell their last names, she just told me to pick one, before moving quickly on to the next student in need of help.

So I was left to sort out my ethnic identity on my own. My definition of what it meant to be Hispanic pretty much came from what I saw on television and in popular culture. According to those rules, I should have bronze skin and dark eyes and speak Spanish fluently. None of that applied to me, so I ended up checking the box marked White.

I wasn't entirely happy with that answer, though, as it didn't seem quite right, either.

I might have had a better and broader understanding of what it means to be Latina if I'd grown up in an area with a large Latino population. But I grew up in southwestern Virginia, an area where native Spanish-speakers were few and far between.

I did speak a little Spanish, but not much. My parents told me that they tried speaking to me in both languages until I was two. At that age, my vocabulary consisted of Mom, Dad, and No. (Perhaps because it's the same in English and Spanish.) My mother was worried that I wouldn't speak at all, so they switched to just English, a decision I've regretted. I've spent years in classes trying to master a language I could have (should have?) learned at home. I couldn't do anything about the way I looked, but if I could speak Spanish fluently, I could feel like I had more of a right to identify myself as Latina. I saw fluency in Spanish as a defense against strangers who told me I didn't "look" Latina.

My childhood wasn't devoid of Peruvian/Latino traditions. My friends and I would take turns swinging a plastic bat in the direction of brightly colored piñatas at my birthday parties. Despite my protests, my head was covered with a *mantilla* for my first communion, and stuffed llamas piled next to teddy bears on my toy shelves.

My mother did most of the cooking, usually fixing typical American fare such as pot roast or mac 'n cheese. But there were exceptions. Occasionally, she'd do Swedish meatballs, or she or my father would cook a Peruvian dish. My favorite food was *arroz tapado*, a dish consisting of rice and a mixture of ground meat, onion, raisins, and hard-boiled eggs. I'd often hover around the stove, inhaling the mouthwatering smells as one of my parents sautéed the onion or sliced the egg.

But as proud as I was of my family and my background, it didn't seem like enough. My life experiences didn't seem tangible enough "proof" that I was Latina.

Perhaps ironically, visits to our family in Peru made me feel even less Latina. I seemed even more of a *gringa* in contrast to my relatives. I'd nod or smile and try to catch the few words I understood as rapid-fire conversations about family or politics in Spanish whizzed between various aunts, uncles, and cousins. Walking around a local grocery store or market I would be acutely aware that my blue eyes and American style of dress marked me as a foreigner.

In high school, which box to check again became an issue as I took my SATs and filled out college and financial aid applications. I wanted to identify as Latina, but still wasn't sure that I had a right to do so. Whenever possible, I would explain my ethnic background and ask if I met the institution's definition of Hispanic.

◆

So I attended the "women of color weekend" with some trepidation. Did I really belong there? Was I a fake, taking a slot away from a "real" Latina?

My fears turned out to be unfounded. Other than the innocuous comment from my hostess, nobody questioned my presence there. I had a great time talking with wonderful women from all over the country. We roller-skated (and fell down) at the rink at the local mall and enjoyed getting to know each other and the school. I felt more comfortable there than at any of the other schools I'd visited and decided to go there in the fall.

When I arrived in September, I was excited to join the Latina group on campus. For the first time in my life, I'd have the opportunity to be part of a Latino community. I arrived early to the first meeting and took a seat on the couch. I smiled at a few of the girls I remembered from the previous spring and started making small talk with the other women there. But after a few polite exchanges, the conversations would die out, and the other girl would excuse herself to go talk with someone else.

I began to feel out of place and self-conscious. It seemed that people were more reluctant to talk to me than the other women there. Was it because I didn't "look Latina"? Or the way I talked? Even though I understood what was being said, I didn't speak "Spanglish" like many of the other women; my conversation was not a breezy mix of the two languages. Normally shy, I made an effort to introduce myself and be friendly, but it didn't seem to be enough. At the next meeting and others that followed, I continued to feel like an outsider. I reluctantly gave up and stopped attending meetings.

I'm still not sure whether I was really unwelcome or whether I projected my own doubts and insecurities onto the other women; probably the latter, although I do remember hearing about one or two other girls having similar experiences with the group.

Nevertheless, college was where I finally became comfortable identifying as both Latina and white. In my women's studies classes, I was introduced to writers like Gloria Anzaldúa and Cherríe Moraga. I learned that I didn't need to be limited by others' definitions or perceptions. Just because I had learned a certain definition of what it meant to be rich or poor, gay or straight, male or female, or Latina or white didn't mean that it was the only one. In class and in my daily life, I learned that there were a lot of gray areas, or borderlands, to borrow Anzaldúa's term. People didn't always fit into neat categories, and how you chose to define yourself was more important than the labels others might place on you.

I became more aware of how encompassing "Latin-ness" can be. One of the most famous Latinas in the twenty-first century is Jennifer Lopez. While I have little in common with the Bronx native (other than a great-grandmother with the surname of Lopez and a butt that's a bit bigger than I'd like), I have tremendous respect for her skills as an entertainer and businesswoman.

An equally talented, if very different, Latina I admire was the late "Queen of Salsa" Celia Cruz. I remember catching a performance of hers one night as I was flipping through channels on the television. While ignorant at the time of the numerous awards and accolades she had received, I was floored and touched by her powerful voice and the *joie de vivre* she radiated through the screen.

I realize how much I've let my own expectations be shaped by the media and others when I'm (pleasantly) surprised to learn that a certain actress or celebrity is of Latin descent, such as "Gilmore Girl" Alexis Bledel or "Wonder Woman" Lynda Carter.

I'm fully aware that for many people I'm not Latina enough and never will be. My skin is too light; my Spanish isn't good enough. But that's okay with me. I know that I'm not any less Latina because I don't meet other people's definitions. I know I'm not less, just different. *Soy latina*, blue eyes and all.

The china cabinet

Jasminne Rosario

OVER EIGHTEEN YEARS AGO my parents came upon a little sum of money my father had saved up after being in the military for two years. One Saturday afternoon, my parents went out and bought both a dining table with chairs and a china cabinet (a.k.a. *El Chinero*) as a set: their first large purchase as a couple. In Spanish, a china cabinet is labeled as a "he," but in my mind our china cabinet has always been a she, because of her delicate yet curvy outer frame and the fragile objects she carries within. Recently, however, after years of torture and instability, the dining room table and chairs have fallen apart and the china cabinet must stand alone, competing for the attention that once so rightly belonged to only her.

It was only just last year that my father finally decided to discard the dining room table and buy a new, luxurious, regally obtrusive larger one. Because I don't live at home with my parents anymore, I was rather appalled when I first saw the new dining table. The new table and the chairs were pretentious and very uncomfortable to sit in. The bulky, dark wood and the sickly flowers that decorated the "cushiony" seats seemed gaudy and out of place in our simple, homely kitchen. Yet my father insists that if it weren't for the new dining table he's so proud of, that he wouldn't feel like "el rey" that he thinks he is. He says that dinnertime is his time, and I guess that the new table adds the last touch to his air of manliness. The old table, like his old job, has been disposed of, and this new piece of solid, sturdy oak wood marks the era of the new life he's always desired.

The china cabinet, on the other hand, means a great deal to my whole family, and it has managed to remain very sturdy, which is probably why it has yet to be replaced. But, it's also important to us because it still carries the memorabilia of all the places we've traveled to and serves as a constant reminder of the many dinners we've shared, while she presided over us with mirror-like reflections of approval. But the cabinet is worn out and I imagine (like myself) rather exhausted from the many times she's moved from one house to another. Together we've moved from the vintage homes in West Point, New York, to the cramped apartment in Germany, and back to the big houses of the South in Tennessee and Texas. Despite all of her travels and many adventures wedged in a moving truck between the loud green couch and my white, rusty metal bunk bed, her glass windows and doors remain surprisingly intact.

On the inside she shines and glitters with sparkling flower vases, overused beer mugs, dusty crystal shot glasses, spoons from around the world, and too many incomplete sets of moldy and deprived wine glasses. She smells of old, wet wood with a faint nauseating mix of Windex and Pine-Sol, like when Grandma had forgotten to shower but continued to religiously apply lotion to her dry and brittle body. Her interior light went out years ago and no one has ever bothered to fix it. Once, we could turn out the lights in the house and see all the beautiful, shiny objects that represented our family's past. Now, however, the objects must sit in their dusty gloom and merely shadow all the other knickknacks we (my mother in particular) have obsessed over and collected throughout the years.

On the outside she looks like someone's old grandmother, waiting to be put away in a home somewhere. Her chipped wood frame and creaking doors echo the sounds of Sugar Hill and Julio Iglesias, crying children and nagging mothers, and the laughter of a family preparing itself to eat a good home-cooked meal.

The china cabinet is very large and very heavy. She's a faded oak color with rusty-gold knobs. The thick glass that has failed to shatter over the years sometimes reflects blue and yellow light against the windows and the walls of our kitchen. And her smooth exterior is often interrupted by water stains in the wood made years ago by forgotten drinking glasses left to perspire on her ledges. Her top half consists of a very creaky door and glass diamond-shaped cutouts. She has two cabinets beneath the glass shelves and three drawers down the middle full of old bills, inactive credit cards, and expired coupons.

The two side cabinets were once opened with a key that only my mother kept. As a child I had always wondered what was in them. I thought Mami had great surprising mysteries that we children couldn't touch. I made up stories of the secret life my mom lived that I believed to be contained in those two drawers. I saw files and folders of all she had ever done, toys from her childhood that even Papi didn't know about, and pictures of all her past lovers and friends who she had left behind. All these thoughts and many others I entertained in my bored imagination. And I knew that there was a real adventure and, hopefully, a great big reward for my hopes when I finally uncovered and opened the door to whatever skeletons the woman once known as "Sonia" had stored up over the years before her body was taken over by the neat freak now known as "Mami."

My chance finally came to uncover all her truths. One day when I was six or seven, while living in Louisiana, I decided to find out what was in the drawers. Mom was in the living room, rearranging curtains and knick-knacks yet again, and I could hear the aching, nostalgic voice of Juan Luis Guerra accompanied by *"una tambora y su guitarra"* playing on the record player, so I knew she was thoroughly distracted. I didn't have the keys because Mami kept those out of reach at all times, but I was a clever and creative child. So I grabbed a kitchen knife and twisted it into the keyhole, until the door finally broke open. I was scared. I didn't know what to expect and I didn't want to get into trouble if she found me. But, I looked anyway. To my disappointment all she had in those drawers were more vases and even more plastic flowers wrapped in newspapers.

I'll never forget that feeling of disappointment mixed with relief that Mami was after all "just" Mom and not Detective Barbie's sidekick. I found nothing of value in those drawers, and many times for many years I would periodically check them to see if there was something worth my while and which would ultimately prove that Mom had served some greater purpose in life. As a child and especially in my early teen years, I sought meaning and the reason for all of our lives being intricately linked by blood, time, and love. I had hoped even as a child to believe that out of all the mothers in the world, Mami was my mom because she was royalty. I sought proof of that hope in those drawers. But there never was anything to prove it.

Mami has lost the keys to the drawers by now, and no one has opened them in years because there's nothing in them. The vases my mom used to keep in there, I found out later, were the ones she'd made herself in pottery classes. Those were her favorites, and because I had a tendency to mysteriously and "accidentally" trip and break anything under four feet high, she had hidden them so that they wouldn't be touched.

Now, when I go back home for vacation, the once cherished vases of my mom and the sturdy china cabinet sit in obscure corners collecting dust and loneliness. They are forgotten emblems of what we held so dear. It's not that my family does not cherish these items, but our lives are changing. We finally live in a stable home, my dad is retired from the military, and we won't be moving or changing homes any time soon. It seems as if there are no more souvenirs to collect.

Everything of value that my parents have collected throughout the years has at one time or another been in that china cabinet. Everything that proves we lived in Germany and Tennessee, New York and Alabama, Texas and Louisiana. All the spoons of all the states we've ever visited and all the mugs, glasses, and plates that represent the one place where we can come together as a family despite everything and enjoy, and sometimes even annoy, each other. The kitchen is our haven, our retreat, and our true home inside the home. As a family, we love to eat and we love to drink. Although the china cabinet now shrinks in the corner compared to the new dining table that seems to have come from another world, in my mind she blossoms with all that remains of our family's older world—hopes and illusions that the new table will never fulfill or erase.

DO YOU SPEAK ENGLISH?

Maritza santibáñez-luna

BORN IN MORELIA, MICHOACÁN, MÉXICO, I grew up only speaking Spanish and celebrating Mexican holidays with my maternal grandparents. My grandmother Magdalena, a housewife, encouraged me the way she wasn't encouraged. Whether we were watching television or eating dinner, I always remember her saying: *"Tú tienes que salir adelante. Vas a ir a la universidad, tendrás una carrera y no dependerás en nadie."* She always smiled when she said this to me, but I always saw the melancholy in her eyes. I knew that this dream had been inside of her for years; she had desired this for herself. Now it was up to me to fulfill the dream that at my age of six was not only my grandmother's anymore.

She and I never thought that one day I would leave my birth country and start all over again in order to find what she believed was an unlimited freedom *y mejores oportunidades*. I arrived at O'Hare Airport in Chicago on a cold January 5th, 1995. My mother lived in Pilsen, one of Chicago's Mexican neighborhoods. Pilsen is what I call *"un pequeño sabor de México en Chicago."* Every business sign is in Spanish and only a few have the English translation; the primary language in the street is Spanish or Spanglish. My mother registered me as soon as possible into a bilingual grammar school. She didn't want me to lose any time and she knew that the transition was going to be a hard one. The first two years of schooling in the United States were not as tough as I thought they would be. Most of my classmates and teachers spoke Spanish, so I was able to communicate with them and not worry about not being able to speak English. The real challenge began when I transferred to a magnet grammar school. Here I was exposed to the diversity of the city of Chicago since the student body was divided between Mexicans, Puerto Ricans, African Americans, and a few whites. Since this new school was not bilingual and none of my teachers spoke Spanish, I had to learn English the hard way with the sink-or-swim method.

I was submerged in an environment that I did not understand. I spent the first year in class not knowing what was going on because I wasn't able to understand or speak the language that was being used. The first day, I was so frightened. I felt so alone. I didn't know anyone. Most of the faces seemed friendly, yet no one spoke to me. I was afraid that the teacher would ask me a question that I wouldn't be able to understand and everyone would laugh at the fact that I did not speak English. So in my desperation of not being laughed at, I approached the teacher and said "I don't speak English," the few words in English that I had learned while studying in Mexico. I had endless afternoons where I was attached to the dictionary looking up the translations of words for my reading class. One assignment used to take me more than four hours to finish. Many days in the classroom and outside of the classroom I felt ashamed, not of my ethnicity but of not being able to learn English fast enough, of not having the correct pronunciation, of not being able to overcome this challenge. My own peers were the cause of this shame and feeling of inferiority. Reading outloud a paragraph from *Willie Wonka and the Chocolate Factory,* I came across laughter from my own classmates. I didn't know that what I thought would help me overcome my fear of speaking English would turn into a nightmare. I started reading and I thought everything was going well, that everyone would applaud my courage, but instead they laughed at my impossibility of pronouncing the word chocolate the same way they did. I never understood why the kids that shared my culture and language laughed at me instead of helping me. It was perhaps because they didn't know what I was going through, how hard it was learning a new language or always being an outsider . . . they didn't know.

Where to go to high school was yet another issue to overcome because the public high schools, at least where I lived in Chicago, were thought of as dangerous and would not get my mother's approval. The neighborhood had only one high school, which was overpopulated and didn't have the funds to create after-school programs to help students prepare for college. There was also the problem with the gangs, violence, and teen pregnancy. Fights almost everyday, cops in every door, and more than thirty students per class. My mother wouldn't let me attend an all-girls Catholic school because she had heard that "there were lesbians there."

Therefore, I attended a co-ed Catholic high school that had just opened in my neighborhood. My mother had a friend whose kid attended the school and mentioned to her that the school had a program where the student would pay for most of his/her tuition by working and that financial aid was also available. After going in for a test, an orientation, and two interviews, I was admitted.

At first I couldn't believe it. I thought they would give preference to those who could pay the tuition, and honestly, my grades were not the best. In this high school, I met wonderful people who believed in me when I didn't believe in myself, but I also met people who still don't believe I've gotten so far, as well as people who simply didn't even know I existed. There were teachers who gave me extra assignments and pushed my capacity because they believed I had potential.

When junior year came, the only colleges and universities that came to talk to us were the community colleges and state universities. Our college counselor at that time never spoke to us about going to school out of state, much less that we could go to an Ivy League institution. I always knew that I wanted to go to college out of state, if possible. I wanted to experience living on my own, making my own decisions, learning how to take care of myself, but having someone near to ask for help if needed. The summer going into my junior year, my boss's daughter, who had graduated from Brown, saw my dedication to school and decided to help me with my college application when I told her I wanted to apply. She told me about the resources that Brown has to offer to their students, the environment that the school has to offer to the student population, and how she met wonderful people who she was still friends with. Hearing her experiences made me fall in love with the school. "Brown is a very good school, but very hard to get into," were her only words of warning to help me from getting disillusioned if I didn't get accepted. What surprises me the most, and now brings a smile to my face whenever someone asks me how I ended up at Brown, is that no one ever told me that Brown University was an Ivy League institution, so popular that it gets about 16,000 applications annually and only admits 1,500 freshmen. That's why I believe that my destiny was to come to Brown University.

I didn't tell many people that I was applying to Brown University, and I never understood why those people who knew were so excited about my decision. My college counselor (a different one at this time) even took me to a counselor who happened to be a priest before going for my interview. When he saw that the priest wasn't able to see us before I left, he quickly took me to the office of the campus ministry director. As soon as we came into his office he shouted, "Maritza is going for her Brown interview. Can you give her a blessing?" and with a smile on his face the director blessed me and wished me the best of luck. I didn't understand the commotion, but I did appreciate the gesture. I didn't know I had applied to an Ivy League college, but if I had known I would have probably not applied. I never thought that an Ivy League college would accept me.

Of course, after everyone in my high school knew that I was their first Ivy League student, everyone knew my name, not necessarily my face or anything else about me, but they knew "Maritza was going to college." Some people even went as far as to say that they had helped me to make my decision to apply to

Brown University. Yet I don't remember anyone specifically saying "apply to Brown" or "apply to an out of state university"; their first concern was to get the majority—if not all—of my classmates to graduate high school. Where we were going to college was an issue that came in second place. I got all the attention after all the work was done, after I already knew that I had choices. Choices that would help me to acquire a better education, that would teach me about myself, and that would give me the opportunity to meet people and learn things that otherwise I wouldn't have.

I had always wondered why friends of mine who were in college all of a sudden dropped out. Now after three years of experience I know the transition to college from high school is hard. Not only is it hard to perform well in the classes if your high school didn't prepare you, many students have to work while in school in order to pay for books and tuition. Also, going from a place where you are the majority to a place where you are the minority can be intimidating.

Having all these disadvantages makes it very difficult to continue, *pero no imposible*. Many cold days walking to a class or from the library to my room, I find myself craving a *champurrado con tamales* or just walking down the neighborhood admiring the murals on the sides of the buildings that paint our struggles *y nuestra esperanza*. That mural showing a family making tamales and enjoying themselves, *la paloma de la paz y la esperanza*, and that girl with her cap and gown and the words *"sí se puede"* underneath it. Many times I wonder what I'm doing here and if Brown is the place for me. But just by looking at people's expressions when I say that I'm a Brown student and knowing that I have inspired other students to "shoot for the stars," as one of my teachers once told me, makes me realize that I belong here.

"Are you Spanish?"

"Do you speak English?"

"There are Latinos in Chicago?"

"What's a Latino?"

The place has changed, but not the questions. These questions will follow me *hasta el fin del mundo* and that's okay, just as long as I know who I am and that my hard work is proof that I belong here.

extranjero
gina taha

IT WAS VERY HARD to accept *un extranjero* (a foreigner) as a father. I had come to a black, colorful neighborhood in New York from Colombia when I was six years old. First grade *extranjeros* taunted me every day, made fun of my lack of understanding, pushed me, stole my school supplies, whispered about me. Physical color had never been important to me, but then I arrived at an unorganized classroom dotted by darker skin tones than my own. *Extranjeros* made me learn another language when I had been perfectly happy with the one I already knew. *Extranjeros* made me cry every day. And daily, when my mother walked me to school in the morning, she would pray *una Ave María* with me so that my day would be different. *Extranjeros* made me hate the Virgin Mary because she never helped me. She never beat up Jane, or struck anyone down dead when they pulled my hair. I guessed that maybe Mary only understood this foreign tongue. I hated this foreign land.

But my mother said she fell in love. She also said she was tired of Latino men, of being treated like a fool, of not being appreciated. There would be no more heavy hands on her face, no more drunken kisses. No one would ever berate her again. I was twelve when my mother introduced us to a tall man with light hair and serious eyes. A white man, because those were the good ones. Once you caught one of those you would be set for life. They loved hot blood and spicy women.

I didn't like the idea of speaking English all the time. I used to get tired of all the syllables and odd letter combinations. Even now, I'd rather speak Spanish and dot my sentences with made-up words. I prefer Latin curses any day; I enjoy hearing a good *¡Carajo!* Back then all I wanted was to laugh in my language and cry in my native tongue. That was gone now. In came this man with his rules and regulations.

Now living in a large humorless apartment made up of white walls and polished floors, I could no longer gossip with my mother in Spanish. It was rude to speak my language when he was around. It didn't matter that I thought quicker in Spanish—now I had to tailor *my* sentences, about *me*, to please a stranger. *"What is she saying?"* I used to love watching my mother brush her long chocolate hair after she got out of the shower, to talk to her about things that were strange to me, about my period, about shaving my legs, about what to do about the cute blond boy at school. No longer was my mother my own. Her time was devoted to trying to keep a household of opposites together. Our time was now timed—everything had to happen when he and his daughter weren't around.

This foreign land had invaded everything that was private about me. I refused to respect this man who every other day reprimanded my mother for loving us. My mother always put her daughters before this man; she thought about our needs before his. In the end, no matter what, we were hers. My sister spent many nights crying in her room when they fought. I would come in to console her, hold her in my lap and whisper Spanish coos, tell her to be strong. Mami loved us even when they quarreled. Some things are unforgettable; hurtful words said out of anger and jealousy have stained me forever. Annoying children, rude children, wouldn't listen to his every command, wouldn't accept him as a father.

It's really hard, nearly impossible, to accept *un extranjero* as a father when there is a constant distinction between the children involved. His blood vs. my mother's. His blond, beautiful daughter vs. his wife's earth-toned children. My sister and I were rich in color, in personality. His daughter, with her cold disposition and unsmiling, blue eyes, was completely devoid of any affection or even friendship.

I tried to rationalize, against my will, that his distinctions were made subconsciously, by mistake. But his differentiations went beyond the way we looked. It was quite apparent that he thought his daughter was better than us. She deserved the best of everything, the first of everything. His golden-haired princess had the best toys, toys that earlier that week we had asked for but had not gotten. When she was around every other week, our everyday existence had to stop and conform to her needs. Dinner was served to her first, with her picking and choosing what she wanted to eat. It seems petty now, but to a twelve and six year old these actions screamed of injustice, of inequality. We wondered if she really was better, if her color meant that she deserved better.

This man fought constantly with my mother about my sister's and my rejection of him as a parental figure, but he didn't deserve being treated as such because he didn't act like a father. A father is supposed to be accepting, understanding, and, most importantly, blind. If he truly wanted to be our father, he would have turned away and ignored our differences, he would have seen past our surfaces. He would have accepted all three of us as children, his just as much as my mother's; he would have seen all three of us as equals. Even if his daughter wasn't our blood sister, it shouldn't have mattered. Yet it always did.

It's hard to accept *un extranjero* as a father when he shows no respect for a child. I never felt stupid asking questions before I met this man. His answer to everything was, "Look it up." Why hadn't I been smart enough to pick up that dictionary to begin with? I had never been taught how to look up something in an encyclopedia, New York City public schooling being what it is. In my imagination I had always believed a good father sat with you and helped you do your homework. I didn't understand a lot of things about this man or his culture. It had to be me, always me. I guessed I was dumb.

There was always a barrier between the stranger in my house and me. I didn't relate to him and he could never relate to me. He would never understand everything I had seen, the things I had felt, all the bad places where I had emotionally traveled. He could never understand what it felt like to be pushed and picked on by a black girl, in a black neighborhood. He didn't know that my father had called me trash and that I could never cry in front of my sister because I had to be strong for her sake. He would never understand why I used to write sad salsa songs at night. He would never be able to read them or understand why my feelings were so intense on paper but not out loud. He didn't speak Spanish and would never understand what *dolor* felt like to me. There was no dictionary to translate that; no encyclopedia would be able to give him the background information on Latin pain. It transcended all time and place; it was too complex for anyone on the outside to understand.

This *extranjero* had no understanding of my mother. Why did she get angry when he only thought about himself? Why would she take his actions toward his daughter personally? Why did she feel hurt when he sided with his ex-wife instead of her? He couldn't comprehend that my mother couldn't afford to be quiet and submissive. She had survived many tumultuous and painful years because she had been strong. Her survival depended on her defensiveness; her kids depended on her instincts. I couldn't understand him. I thought he had fallen in love with her because of the way she was, and, if so, why was her character such a problem now?

I decided that the cute boy with the straw hair and sparsely sprinkled freckles and I would never work out. I made the conscious decision that when I started dating I would never date anyone who was lighter than me or who didn't speak my language. I would never date anyone who couldn't understand my painful salsas. I would never date any *extranjeros*.

sólo Dios sabe

Eusebia Martinez Ulloa

I REMEMBER PULLING UP TO THE DRIVEWAY of my parents' house and feeling a sense of composure. I must have just turned twenty years old and was driving a gleaming teal-blue 1993 Dodge Shadow. As I sat there with my car turned off, I took the time to look around the spacious green yard with the young trees my dad had just planted and the rosebushes my mother had put in. I looked at my father's wood shop and wondered what it was that he kept in there. Sure, there were times when I had seen him building a martin house, a shelf, kitchen cabinets, or a simple varnished UT Longhorn clock with his oversized table saw. However, I had never really paid attention to how the enormous two-story house housing my family of eight came to be and his part in it.

It had all started with my father not wanting to pay the ten-dollar increase in rent for the two-car garage my parents had called their home for a little over a year. The owner of the two-car garage had his house in the front and had made the garage into an efficiency apartment. Dad had originally been paying sixty-five dollars for rent when he decided that no landlord was going to get rich off him. So, as I recall my dad telling the story, his comment to a raise in rent was in his own words. "Bullshit! If I'm going to pay an extra ten dollars a month for rent, why not instead buy a house and at least have something to say is mine?" I must say that even though my dad did not swear nearly as much as my mom, "bullshit" had always been one of his favorite words to use.

So my dad gathered up my newly married mother and his firstborn, newborn daughter named Eusebia and showed us to our new home. The two-bedroom house my dad had bought had a decent-sized yard, a one-car garage, and a fireplace. The house had cost around five thousand dollars, and his mortgage payment was now about one hundred and twenty dollars. I think the price was quite steep considering we lived in the northern part of Texas where it snowed too much to ever leave the house. At least George Strait had made a number-one hit song, in relation to the city no one had ever heard about, called "Amarillo by Morning." I suppose all that mattered was that my dad now had something he could call his own. He would soon have to make an addition to the house.

The idea of a few extra bedrooms, a more spacious kitchen, a larger living room, and a bigger utility room, of course, came with my mother being pregnant for the fourth time. I remember thinking that if she kept getting pregnant at the rate she was going we would one day live in a mansion fit for a king and queen. To this day, I put all the blame on my father for getting my mother repeatedly pregnant. He wouldn't allow her to rest during her childbearing years until one day she bore him a son. I suppose my father made up for it by building my mother and the children bigger houses.

"*Vamos a darle gracias a Dios que* I finally did, *o si no todavía estuviera embarazada con unas veinte hijas chorreadas como ustedes,*" my mother would say. Why my mother called us *chorreadas* I will never know. Perhaps because she was a perfectionist and was always cleaning the kitchen, the living room, or one of the bedrooms. I can still smell the fresh scent of Pine-Sol as I entered the front door of the enormous house. Those are the moments that are retained in my mind because I would always see her holding either a broom or a mop in her calloused, yet delicate hands, making sure the house was spotless.

"*Esta casa es tan grande que* at times when I am here alone with your youngest brother Joseph, I think I hear someone *arri-*

ba. *Yo creo que son* ghosts. *A mí me gustaba* the other *casita in Niederwald más bien. ¿Qué crees tú, Eusebia?"* my mother would ask. The *casita* my mother was referring to had been the second house my dad had built for *la familia.*

I, of course, thought she did not have to bear that many children. The age difference between my brother Joseph and I was already twenty-two years apart. I always told her they would have been fine with just me. But instead she had gone ahead and gotten pregnant on six other occasions. *"¡Qué crees que no más eres tú, huerca chiflada!"* she exclaimed. I guess I had asked for her to yell at me by the remark I had made, but to answer her question, I thought the house in Niederwald was much cozier, warmer, and felt more like a home.

The house my father had built us was in rural Niederwald, a town that consisted of a population of a few hundred people. I thought that by having moved us away from where the cows were slaughtered in desolate Amarillo we would be moving closer to the capital of Texas, not further away from civilization. The closest gas station, restaurant, school, or grocery store was either twenty-five miles to Austin or thirty-something miles going toward San Marcos. The house my dad had just built was in a newly developed subdivision where other new houses were springing up too. But what good was it if nothing was nearby?

Why couldn't we live in the city? Where there were hundreds of shiny tall glass buildings, highways, lots of huge schools, universities, and away from ranches with roaming cows or horses on the pastures. Plus, I always had to call my friends long distance and dad would get irate. I could already see him clenching the phone bill in his large calloused hands and hear his loud, yet stern voice say, "Aaawww, shit, Eusebia, *¿qué son estos números con larga distancia? Chinelas, hombre,* we're going to have to *desconectar el teléfono!"* Then I would really be in for it because my mother's only form of contact with her mother, and her sister, who lived in Florida, was the telephone. I had really dug myself in deep this time. My mother, however, would then end up defending my actions because I was the oldest and about fourteen years old at the time. So, that gave me the right to be able to socialize to some extent.

Saving money had originally gotten my dad thinking in this logical way of never buying a house, but building it himself. I can now relate to all of the tools my father had accumulated through the years in his wood shop that he always kept secret. I have also come to understand how it had served as his own little haven for remembering all the houses he had built for his *familia* throughout the years. It's almost as if my dad had seen the future after seeing his firstborn and predicted that he would one day have a family of eight.

Nine turbulent years have now passed since I sat there in the driveway looking at the house on that peaceful afternoon in May. The immaculate house we all had happily lived in at one time no longer houses *mi familia,* and although our house had been built big enough to fit a king and a queen, my dad had decided to sell his *familia's* beloved house when our queen passed away four years ago. Every now and then, when life is not going so well, I pass by that house and park my car in the driveway. I then start looking at the house and reminiscing about the past times *mi familia* had spent there. I sit there wondering how different *mi familia's* life would have been if my father had not sold the treasured house and can hear my mother saying, *"Sólo Dios sabe, Eusebia. Sólo Dios sabe."*

¿Y todo para qué?

I REMEMBER THE SMOKY, iridescent smell of the church incense and the resonant, comforting sounds of the church bells ringing on a typical Sunday morning. I can still feel how secure I felt as my family sat next to me as Father Peter finished his last sermon at Our Lady of Guadalupe Catholic Church. Throughout mass there would be *alabanzas* that would be sung with such joy and emphasis by everyone in the church. I remember barely reaching my parents' waists in height as I looked up at them as they sang with heart and spirit. Then, within a moment's time, I would get a stern stare as my father clenched his teeth and moved the muscles of his jaw line if I was not participating in the singing of the hymns with them.

I could already hear my dad and my mom lecturing me and staring me down once we would get home. "What kind of *ejemplo* are you setting for your two sisters if you are not going to participate in mass?" he would say. "*Que no sabes* that *Dios* is always watching to see if children are being good or bad, especially in church?" my mother would ask. Sure, I was the oldest of the six children and was supposed to play the role model of a big sister. Nonetheless, half the time it seemed as if I was playing scapegoat for my siblings instead.

I never really got the concept of why we would have to kneel as we came in and then stand up again, and then sit, and then kneel again, and then stand again as we were about to leave. All I know is that when a Catholic is born into the Catholic religion, we are going to follow everything there is from the first sacrament of baptism to the seventh sacrament of extreme unction. A Catholic makes the sign of the cross with holy water as he or she comes into church and prays the holy rosary at the end of mass. There are no questions about it — either you do it or get ridiculed by your parents for not following the traditions outlined by the Catholic faith.

During the last few minutes of mass I would look around at each and every church member as they wore their Sunday best. The women and the girls were dressed in long flowing dresses and nice shiny black shoes. The men and boys were dressed in starched slacks and a black belt with matching polished shoes. There was a strong sense of morals and values denoted as members wore their Sunday best in order to respect the house of the Lord. The children around me were well-behaved and never dared to look at the pew behind them.

Yes, those were the days back in Amarillo, when the girls and women did not wear sandals or dresses that revealed cleavage or the silhouette of their bodies underneath. Now, I feel quite uncomfortable walking into the Catholic Church here in Houston, or even in Austin, and seeing the girls and women dressed in denim shorts or pants that apparently are a few sizes too small for them. Even the boys and men wear denim pants with holes and tears in them. The times have definitely changed from when my classmates and I used to wear socks above our knees with our pleated blue and green school uniforms to Catholic school.

That was the era in which during Holy Communion everyone in the church would have to stay kneeling until a church usher would permit us to get in line to receive the Holy Eucharist. Once everyone had received Holy Communion, we would have to stay kneeling until the priest had proceeded with the mass. The priest would then bless everyone and would finish the mass. Then the *alabanzas* would start again. After the priest had left the church, everyone would gather to greet the priest as we exited the church doors.

However, that was then and this is now. Not one church I have been to since then has practiced the same morals and values I was brought up with. I think it is actually quite disrespectful to leave mass before the priest has even finished. Why can we not all stay kneeling once we have all received the sacrament of Holy Communion and the priest has proceeded with mass?

I now have my own son of five years of age and still cannot comprehend the sexual allegations that have been brought against the Catholic clergy. Growing up in a Catholic family meant that we had a sense of security and confidence as we told our innermost stories and confessions to our priest. A priest is someone we looked up to for having spent half his life studying the Catholic religion and having finalized their ordination sacrament by uniting with God as a servant. I still remember Father Peter as a young Latino with curly black hair who wore glasses and Father Roland with his pale balding head. There was not a time when these priests would not have devoted all of their time in faith and kindheartedness.

What would my loving mother say if she knew this now about the priests we had found so intriguing with their sermons and their character? Priests that were a part of our life. This really does matter to me and holds a great deal of importance to me, considering I can still recall her instilling the magnitude of the priest's role in the Church and the significance of learning our prayers as she would soundly put us to bed at night. She would gently lie me and my two sisters across the strawberry-shortcake sheet on the queen-sized bed. I can still remember the scent of fresh clean laundry as I lay my head across the soft touch of the cotton pillow.

It was then that she would start with all three of us learning to make the sign of the cross. "*En el nombre del . . .*" she would start and then say, "Oh, I forgot no *quieren que hablen en español en la escuela.* So, only in English I will teach you how to pray. Okay." Then she would continue every night teaching us to recite the Lord's Prayer and the Hail Mary.

It has been three years since my young mother passed away and I still feel a sense of urgency to depict the same values that my mother embedded in me as a child to my own five-year-old son. I am now near thirty and decided to move away from my family in Austin about five years ago. My family did not show much interest in having family relations when I did visit from time to time. Therefore, I am now making my life in Houston with my five-year-old son.

However, these kinds of allegations and faults of the priests were never addressed when she was alive. If I was to make a very sincere and educated assumption on behalf of my mother, I am sure that these would be the words I would hear her say regarding the state of disarray I am in regarding priests in the Catholic Church, "I had told you and all of your five brothers and sisters growing up that *el demonio está por donde quiera.* That he can resemble a *persona bonita* or a *persona fea.* He especially looks for *gente* that are *contenta y alegre y que tengan una relación muy cerca con Dios*. Priests are people just like us, and we are not to put them up on a pedestal and adore them as we do God. *No debes de guardar rencor* and move on. Forgive and move on."

Deception

Eliana Vargas

THE PLEASANT FEELINGS IN MY BEDROOM always comforted me. The right side of the large room was my temple, where I always felt the magical sensation of peacefulness. The only drawback was the fact that I shared a room with my older sister. Her cage was on the left side of the room, which was defined by the beige and gold dresser that functioned as the only holy thing separating our distinctive personalities. She was like a giant that furiously stepped on the little people. To her, I was definitely a "little person."

She closely examined the shirt I had borrowed from her. With aggression she ran her skinny, long, inspecting fingers through the pink cotton shirt. She claimed that I had stretched it a size bigger because I was getting fat. Out of nowhere her pathetic voice said I looked like a pig. I had not told her I was pregnant and didn't want her to find out. Her well-defined eyes, covered with eye shadow and mascara, rolled around as if fire were about to explode from them.

My ears were used to hearing her complain about everything I did. "Turn off the radio. I don't feel like hearing anything." Insignificant things always bothered her and we fought constantly over petty things. I followed her commands, especially then when I was pregnant. I was always exhausted and sleepy and did not want to argue with her.

Motionless, I laid on the forest-green carpet with my small skittle-sized belly popping up. As she walked over and stood over my head with her arms crossed, I ignored her. Beyond the fact that we had little communication, I sensed this anger was about more than me stretching her ridiculous shirt. Like a tornado she dropped the question, "Why are you getting married? You're only seventeen."

My emotions were scattered all over the place; a rush of fear entered my body. She too would look down on me. I always claimed to be smarter than her. Yet, that day she finally confronted me, the not-so-smart girl everyone knew me as.

"If you claim to be so smart, why were you so stupid to get pregnant?"

I will never forget those bitter words. I rolled over facing the brittle carpet and slowly was consumed by the darkness of the color. For the first time, in the room where I had always played a role of a warrior, I was shot with an arrow penetrating deep into my heart. Now that I think about it, the truth always hurts.

◆

Happiness overcame all the negative feelings when my fiancé and I looked into all the wedding preparations. Most girls dream about getting married in church. Looking back on it, our parents instilled that belief in us. We looked around at different Catholic churches, but they all required six months of classes before being able to get married. I did not want to wait. If I was going to get married, I wanted everything to be included: the church, the reception, the fun and ecstatic dance, *la víbora de la mar,* and everything else everyone wants on their wedding day. I heard from relatives about one Catholic priest that did not require as much as other churches. I should've realized there was something suspicious about him and that it was too good to be true.

He told us to call him a "Twenty-first-Century Priest." His wisdom and beliefs convinced us to proceed. The wedding would take place in a chapel instead of a church. The chapel was ancient and the white paint chipped away slowly. A large metal arch was in the entrance, lavender-colored silk flowers decorated the small benches. When I asked why he didn't have a church, he said they were in the process of building it. He charged us two hundred dollars, supposedly to pay for the rental of the chapel. He also admitted to not thinking like the other priests and said he did not require six months of advance meetings to marry couples. This priest made me fell alleviated of the sin I carried for being pregnant out of wedlock. He seemed to understand this situation, which sometimes can be so appalling to the Catholic Church. His philosophy was that if two people want to get married, no one has to question that love.

Red shoulder-length hair and a red mustache that reached the corners of his lips proved he was no ordinary priest. When he smiled he looked more like a biker. I clearly remember he was missing more than three teeth. The rest were yellow due to his atrocious smoking habit. Bad breath and dirty yellow stains on his teeth took away the glorified aspect of what a real devoted priest is. All these thoughts rose in my head—an everyday priest does not look like this or carry himself like that. Yet, I still went along with it. After all, who would lie about being a priest? I believed he was truthful.

We were finally married. The disappointment came when we saw Channel 45 and their special news report about a corrupt priest practicing the Catholic religion. Deception and betrayal are the cruelest ways to treat someone. I was victimized by a phony priest. It was all fake. Hundreds of people were victims and a couple gave their testimony on television. Many married couples were immensely hurt. They cried while telling thousands the evil tricks the phony priest had played on them. They mentioned how they would be scarred with this lie for the rest of their lives and how the wedding video and pictures of the church ceremony would bring sadness to them forever. I felt betrayed and gloomy. Yet I was also distressed with myself for not realizing what he really was. I should have gone with my instincts that told me he did not look like a holy priest. But no, I wanted to be married by the Church and wouldn't do it any other way.

I now realize that the bad experience I had not only is a family story everyone can laugh at, but a lesson in my life. To be honest, I was not a truly devoted Catholic. I rarely went to church, but was always made to believe that the only way to achieve maximum happiness in a marriage is to be married in the house of God. Now, sitting here today I have witnessed that love is what really counts in a marriage. The truth is that I was married by God, I believe in God, and He will oversee my happiness and bless me and my family every day of my life.

I don't care anymore what my family will say, even though one of the factors in the reasoning of why I decided to get married so young was due to my family's comments and reactions, especially those of my sister. I have overcome the situation of being young and immature. Also, I had the nerve to put a stop to the little girl I was, who always tried to please the family. I'm happy to be married and to have the child who brought this life lesson.

When I look at our wedding video and pictures, I don't see that fake priest and the cruelty behind his actions. I see our hands held tight and the reflection of our love. Our shining eyes gleaming at each other by the wonderful water fountain in the Galleria. A remembrance of our souls uniting together by the glorified action of love that I hope will last an eternity.

My Mexico City Grandpa
Monica Leticia Velasco

HE SEES THE BEAUTIFUL GIRL walk through the store and their eyes lock at once for two seconds, but he looks away, sighing deeply because he knows that it will be difficult for him to court a widow. She comes again the next day, strolling confidently in her navy blue heels with a matching suit and clutching a purse in her silk gloves. But this time she does not look for her groceries; instead, she walks directly to him with eyes fastened on his. His excitement grows; all he can do is smile a big and welcoming smile, thinking that this attractive brunette with irresistible curls is interested in talking to him. His dream will come true because love found him. . . .

The woman in the blue suit and the man with the nicely combed hair and friendly smile have engaged in a pleasant conversation that begins their first of many conversations, foreseeing their future. Love found my grandfather and grandmother and their passion surpassed their friends' and families' hurtful words. Moreover, my grandmother was insulted, judged an outcast by 1950s society. Family members and friends grimaced over my grandmother's love for my grandfather, even though she had already lost her first husband and my grandfather was seven years younger. Yet, they got married on May 31, 1953, after giving birth to four children. My grandfather still sees her sixty-one years later in everyone's smiles and in his thirty-eight-year-old parrot's squawking to her. He now sits hunched over the window looking out at a beautiful bright sunny day in Mexico City, holding a picture of his deceased used-to-be-navy-blue-dressed devotion in his wrinkled, aging hands.

My grandfather's spirit for life reminds me what Latino means to me. Latinos are charismatic people who allow life to unfold into fiery enchiladas verdes, guitar-playing festivities with swaying hips and arms to the beat of tango, merengue, salsa, and contagious laughter that brings crinkly and tear-eyed smiles together with witty Spanish jokes. Latinos are love—our personality adds magical charm to the manner in which we unmask our way of life. Cozy and inviting, Latinos capture others by passion and humor.

I can see all of these qualities in my grandfather and how his infinite wrinkles are not enough to calculate how life and love came to him. It is his heartfelt smile, patience, and carefree energy that have inspired me. My aspiration is to share my beliefs of contentment and love with others as my grandfather demonstrated to me through his perpetual love for my late grandmother and his contagious exuberant charisma.

It is my grandfather and my many visits to Mexico City —noisy and overcrowded, full of aromas of *chile* and *cilantro*— that has defined my Latino personality. The Mexico City nightlife is not always boisterous; there are also peaceful cafés. Both the serenity of a relaxed café and the upbeat, noisy lifestyles full of warm and peppery cooking are satisfying images that remind me of Mexico City.

Despite the drooping, humble, and wrinkled eyes, my eighty-two-year-old grandfather still manages to put forth his energy in repetitive jokes and humorous stories.

The definition of my Hispanic background all comes down to this: when love finds us we take everything and sacrifice anything to embrace love, smile, and to please others. Consequently, my family has always taught me to live life to its fullest and appreciate everything I have. Being able to witness my contented grandfather laugh and influence others helps me to be more optimistic and devour this Latino culture. My Mexican culture has also taught me discipline, to eat spicy foods, how to dance, and to always laugh. These characteristics remind me of the way Latinos are because they seem to give off a relaxed and positive charisma. I am also the person I am today because I have been able to visit my family in Mexico City and relive the experiences of a big family like the one in "My Big Fat Greek Wedding." My family has an overwhelming love for life and one another that greatly exceeds their flaws.

I wonder how someone can live and love as much as my grandfather loves. When asked what my Latino background is to me, I am reminded of him, the man who has inspired many. His genuine happiness envelops me. My Mexican descent has given me a life of music and laughter, the smells of spices, and sights of welcomed smiles, which I call "the little things" I love. These "little things" and the way love came to my grandfather have inspired me profoundly to appreciate my heritage.

our family secret
teresa zuñiga

WHEN I WAS GROWING UP, birthdays at my grandmother's house were huge affairs. My grandmother's entire neighborhood would be put on notice that the Ortiz's were having a party when the melodic voice of José Alfredo Jiménez blared all the way down the block. Most of my grandmother's neighbors didn't mind because they were usually in attendance. There would be long, mismatched tables covered with white paper tablecloths set up in the shaded backyard that would groan under the weight of bottomless aluminum platters and brightly colored bowls of barbecue, tamales, rice, beans, potato salad, and mole. Mountains of tortillas would be placed at each end of the table, waiting for hungry hands to pass them around. It seemed as if anyone and everyone with the last name of Ortiz in the city of Houston would show up to eat, show off baby photos, play dominos, and quietly criticize someone's cooking. People that I hadn't known existed would come over and plant wet kisses on my sister and I, then slyly comment about how much we resembled my dad's side of the family, as if it was a cause for lamentation. The only thing that made all this bearable was the anticipated entertainment that took place at every Ortiz family function. I didn't know at the time that my much-loved entertainment was the family's biggest secret.

My Uncle Adam was always the center of attention at family gatherings, especially with the grandchildren. We loved that he would always volunteer to entertain the thirty-something of us in order to keep us out of mischief. Our parents would gladly grant him temporary custody of the children so that the women could cook and gossip in peace and the men could gather outside around a cooler filled with six-packs of Pearl beer and spit out statistics proving their stance about which Texas professional football coach was better—the Dallas Cowboys' Tom Landry or the hometown hero, Bum Phillips of the Houston Oilers. While all this was going on, Uncle Adam would make his usual big production of congregating us into my grandmother's big brown living room. He would sit on my grandfather's patched tapestry recliner, and beneath the many black-and-white portraits of mean-looking people, he would tell us jokes and the most amazing stories. Tales of restless ghosts that were doomed to haunt the bad people of the world would capture everyone's attention. We would all be entranced by the mock terror in his expressive, hazel eyes that contrasted with his mocha skin. His long, thin face would contort in different ways as he spewed out each haunting detail. Then, just when he knew he had us all on the edges of our seats, he would turn the horror story into a big joke by finishing it off with a conclusion so outrageous that we would end up in hysterical laughter. Everyone would be laughing, except for one person, his son.

My older cousin, Adam Jr., was a contradiction in character to his father. Though he was tall and slender like his dad, he hadn't inherited his father's gregarious manner or his sense of humor. He was a loner and always seemed to be in a foul mood. During his father's story time, Adam Jr. was usually brooding somewhere in a corner. Because of this, I made it a point to avoid him. It was not until years later, when we were both adults, did I find out about the burden that he had been forced to carry.

As irrational as it now sounds, my uncle was most famous among us kids for his ability to drink several cans of beer without taking more than one breath in between each one. Having seen this so many times, we knew that after the fourth or fifth can, he would stand up and pretend to fall. Occasionally, he would say something foul about one of our parents or let a curse slip out, which would bring choruses of giggles from those of us sitting among crushed beer cans. Profanity was nothing new to us. It was part of my Aunt Lila's everyday language. She had turned it into an art form, with the talent of stringing together four-letter words, in both Spanish and English, as if they were beads on a necklace. However, for the younger generation, profanity was a crime that would result in swift and humiliating punishment. As my uncle drank more, he would become louder and more belligerent. His tales would become increasingly darker and often include one of his drinking buddies or some woman he had met at a bar. This would continue until one of our fathers would come in and "put a stop to it." "Putting a stop to it" usually entailed the grandchildren being sent outside to play, while my uncles and my father had a "discussion" with him about responsibility and common sense. Unfortunately, these "discussions" would always end in the same way. My uncle would get angry, curse everyone out, and leave. His wife, my Aunt Ofelia, who had learned by experience to come in a separate car, would gather up Adam Jr. and his siblings, shuffle them out the front door with as little commotion as possible, and collect her things to leave. Her departures were often accompanied by a series of mumbled apologies to my grandmother for the disrespecting of her house and then to those whom my uncle had offended. There would be offers to help her haul her bowls and kids to the car, but she would always refuse. It was as if the refusal was her only way of keeping what was left of her dignity intact. With downcast eyes, she would hurry out the door and down the porch steps to the blank stares of my cousins who were waiting by their car. They were used to the routine. From behind my grandmother's prized pink and yellow rosebushes, I would sometimes watch them quietly climb into their blotchy blue station wagon and drive away. It was strange to me that no one would mention the situation or my uncle again for the rest of the day. If I asked one of my parents about him, I was usually given a stern look or told to stay out of "adults' business." Over time, I accepted this and didn't ask.

When Uncle Adam died in 1997 from liver cancer, there was an enormous expression of mourning at the funeral from the entire family, except for one. Adam Jr. had chosen not to attend the funeral. I was curious. Several weeks later, Adam Jr. and I met and he shared our family's secret with me. He told me that his childhood had been devastated by his father's never-ending series of drunken stupors and extramarital affairs. The entertainment that we, as children, looked so forward to at family gatherings was a part of his everyday life. My uncle's "act" of profanity and abusive behavior was real in their household, but Adam was forbidden to speak about it with anyone outside his immediate family. It was considered inappropriate or disrespectful for the children to speak openly about adult issues, even if they were directly affected by them. As a result, Adam Jr. spent much of his teenage years angry with his father and our extended family. It infuriated him that we laughed at his misery and that our parents ignored it, even after Aunt Ofelia pleaded with them to intervene. He told me that it had been just in the past two years that he had been able to confront some of his anger issues. He had joined a children of alcoholic parents support group and, through their counseling, he had begun to deal with his relationship with his father. His group gave him the courage to love his father despite the fact that he was still angry with him. He told me that he had once tried to get his father to attend a group meeting with him and my aunt, but he had refused. Uncle Adam blamed his son's problems on my aunt's "constant babying" and wanted no part of him or his "therapy." After that, Adam Jr. said his father refused to see or speak with him. It was almost eight months before he saw his father again in the hospital. The doctors had advised my aunt to call the family together. He said that his mother pleaded with his father to make peace with him, but up until the moment that he died he refused to acknowledge or apologize for all the pain that his alcoholism had caused them. Adam Jr. said his father died angry, just as he had lived.

Adam Jr. told me that he couldn't bring himself to attend the public funeral. He said that there was so much he needed to say to his father, but he couldn't do it in front of anyone. The evening of the funeral, after everyone had gone home, he went to the burial site with the intention of cursing his father's body, memory, and the secret that he made the family keep. He said he knew exactly what he was going to say. He was going to hurt his father like he had hurt him all his life. As he sat in his car, looking at the mound of freshly shoveled dirt, he said he began to cry uncontrollably. All the pain that had been locked up inside of him for twenty-nine years gushed out as the reality of his loss set in. His father was gone and the burden of the secret with him.

Adam Jr. was married last November. It had been a long journey for him since the death of his father. Seven months after his father's funeral, he left Houston for two years to "learn to be his own man." Upon his return, he settled into a job and continued attending support group meetings, but he distanced himself from all but a few members of the family. After three years of living a solitary existence, he found happiness. Gloria, a woman he met at his support group, understood him in a way that few did. She had not only grown up with an alcoholic mother, she had also once been married to one. He said that she and her fourteen-year-old son had taught him how to laugh again and not be so cynical about the world around him. Though he was scared of making the same mistakes with his stepson that his father had made with him, he was also excited about the prospect of having a family that he could love unconditionally. In addition, he could help his new stepson deal with the same issues, concerning his father, that he had struggled with all his life. Adam Jr. said that his stepson needed to know that he wasn't responsible for his father and that his DNA didn't determine what type of man he would grow up to be. A man's character is judged by the content of who he is during his journey, not who he is at the end of it.

TO BE an oʀtIz

"BROTHERS AND SISTERS, family, friends, and loved ones, we gather today to lay our brother, Phillip Ortiz, to rest. As a beloved and faithful husband, father, and friend, Phillip affected the lives of all who met him. He will be truly missed, but the world has been made a better place because he was here."

As the aged and withered reverend slowly spoke, I thought of how odd it was to hear him call Chato by his birth name. Although he was twenty-two years older than I, and at the time of his car accident had three children, two of whom were also older than I, he had always been "Chato" to me. In fact, his nickname was so familiar to everyone in the family that even his parents and his wife used it. That was part of the gift that my uncles gave to him and the rest of the Ortiz grandchildren—a legacy in the form of a family tradition that supersedes everything, even the grave.

◆

The Ortiz legacy was begun many decades ago by my infamous uncles: Adam, Abel, and Roland. My mother's older brothers took a great deal of perverse pleasure in giving all the Ortiz grandchildren nicknames that the rest of the family would eventually pick up and would stay with us for all of our natural lives. The family treated this practice as some type of holy sacrament that would bring a swift and horrifying retribution if not performed. I once asked my mom why we had this strange ritual. She said it was "the power of *familia*."

◆

When I look back on the christening of my immediate family's nicknames, I realize that my sister and I were fortunate. My uncles were not as malicious to us as they were to my other cousins. Some of my cousins were christened Booger, *El Chango* (monkey), *La Princess, La Güera* (light-skinned), *El Pico* (named for his nose), the Titty-Baby, and El Mighty

Mouse. In our case, my uncles thought that it was hilarious that I was chubby and my older sister Cindy was very thin. The story behind both our nicknames was that the moment they saw me, they called me "Gordy," which was short for *gordita* (chubby). They called my sister *La Flaca* (thin one). I was told some years ago that for a short time, when I was three and Cindy was five years old, the running joke in the family was that my parents had the "before and after" twins. This went on until the day of my cousin Goun-Goun's wedding reception, when my father pulled aside two of my uncles and quietly and politely told them that the joke was over. After that, it was never told again—at least not in front of my parents, my sister, or me.

Throughout my early grammar school years, I believed that my uncles were the meanest men who walked the earth. I imagined an evil in them that rivaled even the worst villains in my favorite Saturday morning cartoons. They even nicknamed their own kids, as my Uncle Roland did with Chato. Nevertheless, my mother would always tell me that I just did not understand them. As insane as it sounds, through time I learned that this was how my uncles showed their love for us. When my grandfather died at the age of forty-nine of a heart attack, the responsibility of the family fell upon his sons. Despite the fact that they were only sixteen, seventeen, and nineteen years old, they took the title of being the "men of the house" seriously. For my mother and her younger siblings, they were the anchors of the family, both financially and emotionally.

In the 1950s, Latino families were dominated by a strong patriarchal system that adhered to the legend of the ultimate boys' club: Machismo. Membership into this club involved a lifelong commitment to social and cultural boundaries that were to be strictly followed, despite circumstances, eras, or those involved. My uncles were the children of a generation that reveled in this legend. It was a generation full of Jorge Negrete's "México Lindo," *Fiestas Patrias* celebrations that meant more than a beer commercial, extended families living on the same block, and the belief that the man of the house was in charge. As young Latino males, my uncles were indoctrinated to believe that it was a sign of weakness in their character for them to show any sentimental emotion. Heartache, regret, love, affection, and especially tears were all to be kept private. *Machistas* would have a bar brawl over a bottle of cheap beer before they would tolerate a brother being seen as crying over a broken heart. It was almost like a form of self-preservation for Latinos. In the era of wars, a presidential assassination, counterculture movements, and civil rights marches, Machismo afforded them a method for preserving themselves both culturally and ethically. My uncles accepted their place in the Machismo legend and consecrated it until it surpassed being a part of their culture and became part of their very character.

I remember another funeral three winters ago. Despite the fact that the November day was cold and rainy, my uncles wore dark sunglasses so no one could see their red, puffy eyes. Throughout the entire burial service, they stood emotionless, like stone statues on the worn, green carpeting behind my aunt's cold metal chairs. They neither bowed their heads nor sought solace from the heavens. They merely stared straight ahead as if they were waiting for my grandmother to rise up out of the mahogany box. Occasionally, one of them would quickly wipe away a tear or blow his nose into the white, monogrammed handkerchiefs that they all carried. I knew that the loss of my grandmother had devastated them. Throughout their entire lives, she had been their steadfast encourager, supporter, and teacher. She had taught them how to respect our culture, our families, and themselves. My uncles were allowed to make their own mistakes and to learn from them. She gave them the opportunity to grow into the men that they now are. As a result, they held her in high esteem and demanded that the rest of the family do the same. Disrespect toward my grandmother was an unwritten crime and retribution for those who broke it was swift and severe. Now she was lost to them; their first love was gone. I knew that pain was welling up inside of them, but their resolve to stay strong for the family took precedence. They chose to hold up the family as opposed to being upheld. I believe that this is what helped them work through their pain and continue with their lives.

As an adult, I now understand that the nicknames my uncles gave us were the products of their attempts to preserve the cultural and familial bonds that they were given. The absurdity of the names were only a ruse to mask the deep caring that they felt for each of us. As my mother once tried to explain to me when I was a child, the power of *familia* was what inspired past generations to survive and surpass economic depressions, blatant racism, and devastating losses. These bonds are what gave them strength, security, and a sense of identity that could only come from a strong family. Thanks to my uncles, these bonds of *familia* have been passed on, not only to my generation but to the subsequent one as well. I know that no matter where we go, who we marry, or how old we become, we will always have our family. It is the power of my *familia* that drives me and will make me succeed.

contributors' bios

The second of three first-generation Mexican-American girls, **Nancy L. Avila** was born and raised in Houston, Texas, where she attended the University of Houston, majored in English literature, and became certified in secondary education. She currently teaches high school Freshman English and continues to share her love of reading and writing with young and eager minds, hoping to do for them what so many wonderful teachers did for her.

Georgina Baeza was born in Ciudad Juárez, Chihuahua, Mexico. At the age of one, she and her family immigrated to El Paso, Texas, the sister city of her birthplace. She has completed a BA in English literature at the University of Houston.

Claudia Balderas was born in Reynosa, Tamaulipas, Mexico. She is currently a senior at the University of Houston and is working on a bachelor's degree in Spanish to become a Spanish high school teacher.

Maria Teresa Brothers Maria Brothers was born in Zihuatanejo, Guerrero, Mexico. At the age of eighteen, she moved to Houston, Texas. She completed a BA with a minor in English at the University of Houston in 2004.

Nicaraguan by descent, Californian by birth, and Texan by default, **Aisha Jara Calderon** currently calls Houston her home. Being blessed with a childhood that embraced two cultures, she constantly finds new ways to incorporate both into her art. Her love of photography and writing allow her to relish new social situations where everything can eventually be captured through either medium.

A Congressional Prize-winner in her home country of Honduras, **Melissa Cantor** is a recent graduate of the MFA program in creative writing at the University of Miami. Depending on when you track her down, she works as a freelance writer, magazine editor, composition teacher, and fiction workshop leader.

Adam Castañeda is a sophomore at the University of Houston majoring in English with a minor in Asian American studies. He is the recipient of a National Scholastic Writing award and has been published three times in *Teen Ink*. Adam enjoys film, music, and musical theater as well as socializing with friends and learning about different cultures.

Dalia Cruz is an English major, currently classified as a senior at the University of Houston. She is of Mexican-American descent and the oldest, and only, sister of three brothers.

James Espinoza was born in Los Angeles and raised in California's Central Valley, where he grew up watching Sábado Gigante and working at swap meets. He received his BA from Loyola Marymount University and is currently pursing an MFA in creative writing at California State University, Fresno.

Nick Gaitan was born in and lives in Houston, Texas. He attended the University of Houston for his bachelor's degree in English. He also performs, playing upright bass in Houston as well as other parts of the country on tours with an independent musical group, Los Skarnales.

Cristina A. Gomez was born in McAllen, Texas, and is a graduate of the University of Houston. An art enthusiast, she hopes to earn her master's in arts administration.

Jynelle A. Gracia is a MFA candidate in the University of Iowa's nonfiction writing program.

Valarie Hurtado is Mexican American. Currently she is a senior at the University of Houston, majoring in psychology and minoring in Mexican American studies. When she graduates she plans on attending graduate school and focusing on child/adolescent psychology.

Yvonne Flores Lemke lives in Katy, Texas, with her husband Joseph. She is currently an ESL teacher for Katy Independent School District. She received a BA in English from the University of Houston in 2004. She is a Mexican American.

Marisol León is a Mexican-American Chicana, born and raised in Los Angeles, California. She currently attends Yale University, where she cultivates her passion for writing, traveling, and social justice. She plans to pursue a journalism career and/or go into diplomacy.

Flor López graduated from the University of Houston in the Fall of 2004.

Juan Macias was born in the beautiful port of Tampico, Tamaulipas, Mexico. On October 1, 1995, he entered the United States of America hand-in-hand with his mother and kid sister. He takes pride in being a native Mexican candidate for the Bilingual International Baccalaureate Diploma.

Annette Teresa Martinez was born and raised in Houston, Texas. She currently teaches secondary English and is working toward her master's degree.

Rosaura L. Martinez was born in Monterrey, Mexico. After living there for nine years, she moved into her father's house and lived there for eleven years. She attended Stafford High School and graduated in May 2002. She attends the University of Houston–Central Campus.

Victor Matsumura was born in Mexico City. He is of Japanese descent from his father's parentage and Native American and Mexican from his mother's ancestry. He currently attends the University of Houston as a photography major.

Gabriel Medina attends the High School for the Performing and Visual Arts in Houston, Texas. He has been playing the piano for almost twelve years and plans to live his life as a musician. He is a two-time recipient of the top-ranking in the University Scholastic League State Competition, as well as the winner of the 2005 International Chopin Youth Competition.

Perla Melendez reads, writes, and hula-hoops, though not all at the same time, in her dorm room at the University of California–Santa Barbara, where she is a second-year Literature and Book Arts double major in the College of Creative Studies. She is a native of Los Angeles.

Alicia Montero is a Mexican-American borderland dweller. She finished her undergraduate education at the University of Notre Dame and is pursuing a masters at the University of Texas at Austin's Creative Writing Program. As a child, when asked what she wanted to be when she grew up, she always said she wanted to be a swan.

Juanita Montoya is a native Houstonian and is currently a student at the University of Houston. She is majoring in English with a concentration in creative writing and hopes to one day be a high school English teacher and to continue writing.

Melissa A. Moran is a graduate from the University of Houston, where she majored in creative writing and minored in Mexican American studies. She also has received her certification in teaching and is currently a first grade bilingual reading teacher at Galena Park ISD.

Génesis Piña is a 23-year old Dominican, born and raised in New York City, Washington Heights. She graduated from the City University of New York–Hunter College with a double major in creative writing and media studies. Currently, she works as a business coordinator for Latin America.

Remy Ramirez was born in Austin, Texas. As both her parents were artists, she quickly became interested in her own forms of expression, pursuing writing and dance avidly by the time she was ten years old. She later graduated from the University of California–Santa Barbara with a degree in literature, and a minor in Spanish and is currently pursuing her masters in creative writing at the University of Texas at Austin.

Evelin Rivera is currently a senior at the University of Houston. She is twenty-five years old. She was born in El Salvador and came to the United States when she was eight years old.

E. M. Rodriguez is of Swedish-Peruvian (as well as Italian and Spanish) descent, and likes people and things that don't fit into neat categories. She graduated from college with a degree in women's studies and a minor in Spanish in 2002.

Jasminne Rosario is currently a graduate student attending the University of Houston, hoping to receive a masters in education in the near future. Although she has grown up all around the United States, she comes from a Hispanic family of the Dominican Republic. She is pursuing a career in teaching and, maybe, even writing.

Maritza Santibáñez-Luna was born in Morelia, Michoacan, Mexico. She was raised by her maternal grandparents and migrated to Chicago in January of 1995. She graduated from Brown University in May 2006, the first of her family to receive a college degree.

Having graduated with honors from the Fashion Institute of Technology, **Gina Taha** is of Colombian and Palestinian descent and now resides and works in New York.

Eusebia Martinez Ulloa is a Latina of both Spanish and Mexican descent. She was born in Amarillo, Texas. She graduated in the fall of 2005 and plans to utilize her degree to make an impact on the lives of the population of Latinos dropping out of high school.

Eliana Vargas is a Mexican American who is the first to attend college in her family. She graduated in May 2006 with a BA in psychology from the University of Houston. She is a member of the National Honor Society of Psychology.

Monica Leticia Velasco grew up in Houston, Texas, but was born in Mexico City, Mexico, on September 21, 1987. She graduated from St. Agnes Academy High School. Art and defending people's rights fascinates her, which is why she wants to attend the University of Texas at Austin to become a successful lawyer.

Teresa Zuñiga is a native of Houston, Texas. She received her BA in English and a minor in Mexican American Studies from the University of Houston. She is currently working on a young adult novel, a nontraditional chronicling of life in Houston's East Side.